The NEW
ELEMENTARY SCHOOL LIBRARIAN'S ALMANAC

BARBARA FARLEY BANNISTER

**THE CENTER FOR APPLIED
RESEARCH IN EDUCATION**
West Nyack, New York 10995

With love to Jeffrey, Erin, Jeremy,
Dustin, Nikki, Samantha, and Craig

10 9 8 7 6 5 4 3

Library of Congress Cataloging-in-Publication Data

Bannister, Barbara Farley.
    The new elementary school librarian's almanac : practical ideas,
tips, techniques, and activities for every month of the school year
/ Barbara Farley Bannister.
        p.   cm.
    Includes index.
    ISBN 0-87628-605-8
    1. Elementary school libraries—Activity programs.   2. Elementary
school libraries—Calendars.   3. School year—Calendars.   I. Title.
Z675.S3B236 1991
027.8′222—dc20   91-252
                                                                    CIP

**The Center for Applied
Research in Education**
Business Information Publishing Division
West Nyack, NY 10995.

Simon & Schuster. A Paramount Communications Company

PRINTED IN THE UNITED STATES OF AMERICA

ACKNOWLEDGMENTS

Thanks to Jan Carlile, Adams School Librarian, for some of the ideas for hosting an author, and for the ideas on bibliographies. Thanks also to Cindy Stinson-Chennell, Columbus School Librarian, for the idea of the READ-AWAY AIRLINES reading program.

ABOUT THE AUTHOR

Barbara Farley Bannister has been the library media specialist at Memorial Elementary in McMinnville, Oregon, for seventeen years. Before that, she taught kindergarten, second grade, third grade, and fifth grade. The author of numerous books, library skills games, puppet scripts, and more, her previous books for The Center include **Library Media Center Activities for Every Month of the School Year, Reading Round-Ups,** and **Reading Bingos, Puzzles and Research Activities for Every Month of the Elementary School Year.**

Ms. Bannister earned her B.A. from Western Michigan University in Kalamazoo and did graduate work at Portland State University and Western Oregon State College. She is married and has four children and seven grandchildren. The poetry and art in this book are her own.

There is nothing like returning to school after a restful summer, smelling the freshly waxed floors, and feeling again the mingled apprehension and excitement of beginning a new year. *The New Elementary School Librarian's Almanac* will help you make sure that the year will be happy, constructive and exciting. Organized by the month, it places in your hands a wide variety of ideas and activities, as well as ready-to-use forms, activity pages, and patterns that you can use to make your library and media center (LMC) a stimulating place that students will use and enjoy. Each month, the *Almanac* offers

- a calendar of birthdays and anniversaries
- suggested themes for the month
- instructions for special days and activities
- bulletin board ideas and ready-to-use patterns
- activities for a monthly Authors Birthday Club
- a variety of contests for the contest corner
- suggestions for an arts and crafts corner
- research activities for the nonfiction corner
- library skills lessons and activities
- recommendations for storytimes and book talks
- LMC management tips and forms.

A special section in September helps you get off to a good start, with information about enlisting volunteers and student aides and planning the year ahead of time. In June, you will find tips on getting materials back in the library *and* inventoried and a summer reading program you can set up with minimal effort. Throughout the year, you will find survival tips for inevitable issues that range from computerizing the library to dealing tactfully with unwelcome donations from the public. You will also learn how to keep in touch with classroom teachers and get support from your administrator. The *Almanac* is *not* designed to sit on your shelf and should be a continuous help to you as you plan how to make your library an attractive, welcoming place throughout the school year. And because ideas often generate more ideas, there are numerous places for you to write in your own brainstorms, favorite activities, and more, to make this your own personal planning guide.

I hope that you will use this book for many years to help you create a happy and functional LMC.

Barbara Bannister

TABLE OF CONTENTS

About This Resource iv

SEPTEMBER

    September Calendar • 2
    Special Tasks for September • 3
        Magazines • 3
        Catalogs • 3
        New Materials • 3
        Setting Up Special Areas • 4
        Scheduling Audiovisual Equipment • 5
        Scheduling Classes • 5
        Preparing an Overall Plan for the Year • 6

    September Themes • 6
    Special Days in September • 9
    September Bulletin Boards • 10
    September Authors Birthday Club • 11
    September Contest Corner • 17
    September Arts and Crafts Corner • 19
    September Nonfiction Corner • 20
    September Skills Classes • 21
        Orientation Classes • 21
        Other Skills Classes • 22

    September Storytimes • 24
    September Book Talks • 26
    LMC Management • 27
        Parent Volunteers • 27
        Student Volunteers • 27

    September Patterns • 33

OCTOBER

    October Calendar • 38
    October Themes • 39
    Special Days in October • 40
        Dictionary Day • 40
        Teddy Bear Day • 40
        Teddy Bear Tags • 41

    October Bulletin Boards • 42
    October Authors Birthday Club • 43

October Contest Corner • 46
October Arts and Crafts Corner • 46
October Nonfiction Corner • 48
October Skills Classes • 51
October Storytimes • 51
October Book Talks • 55
LMC Management • 58
  Overdue Books • 58
  Audiovisual Training • 58

October Patterns • 60

NOVEMBER

November Calendar • 66
November Themes • 67
Special Days in November • 67
November Bulletin Boards • 69
November Authors Birthday Club • 70
November Contest Corner • 72
November Arts and Crafts Corner • 73
November Nonfiction Corner • 74
November Skills Classes • 75
November Storytimes • 78
November Book Talks • 78
LMC Management • 79
  Audiovisual Check-Out Management • 79
  Ordering • 80

November Patterns • 81

DECEMBER

December Calendar • 84
December Themes • 85
Special Days in December • 85
December Bulletin Boards • 86
December Authors Birthday Club • 87
December Contest Corner • 89
December Arts and Crafts Corner • 90
December Nonfiction Corner • 92
December Skills Classes • 94
December Storytimes • 94
December Book Talks • 95

LMC Management • 96
   Author's Visit • 96

December Patterns • 98

JANUARY

January Calendar • 102
January Themes • 103
   Fantasyland • 103
   Fairy-tale Newspaper • 104

Special Days in January • 105
   Martin Luther King, Jr. Day • 105
   Other Days • 105

January Bulletin Boards • 105
January Authors Birthday Club • 107
January Contest Corner • 109
January Arts and Crafts Corner • 109
January Nonfiction Corner • 112
January Skills Classes • 113
January Storytimes • 115
January Book Talks • 117
LMC Management • 118
   Keeping in Touch with Teachers • 118

January Patterns • 119

FEBRUARY

February Calendar • 126
February Themes • 127
Special Days in February • 127
February Bulletin Boards • 128
February Authors Birthday Club • 129
February Contest Corner • 131
   Memorize Something Patriotic • 132

February Arts and Crafts Corner • 133
February Nonfiction Corner • 133
February Skills Classes • 134
   Finding Quotations • 134
   Research Contest • 136

February Storytimes • 138

February Book Talks • 140
LMC Management • 141
   Card Filing • 141
   Weeding • 141

February Patterns • 143

MARCH

March Calendar • 146
March Themes • 147
Special Days in March • 147
March Bulletin Boards • 148
March Authors Birthday Club • 150
March Contest Corner • 150
March Arts and Crafts Corner • 152
March Nonfiction Corner • 152
March Skills Classes • 153
   Publishing Books • 153

March Storytimes • 155
March Book Talks • 156
LMC Management • 157
   Book Fairs • 157

March Patterns • 159

APRIL

April Calendar • 164
April Themes • 165
Special Days in April • 165
April Bulletin Boards • 166
April Authors Birthday Club • 167
April Contest Corner • 169
April Arts and Crafts Corner • 170
April Nonfiction Corner • 170
April Skills Classes • 171
April Storytimes • 176
April Book Talks • 177
LMC Management • 178
   Donated Books and Magazines • 178

April Patterns • 181

MAY

May Calendar • 186
May Themes • 187
Special Days in May • 187
May Bulletin Boards • 187
May Authors Birthday Club • 189
May Contest Corner • 189
May Arts and Crafts Corner • 191
May Nonfiction Corner • 192
May Skills Classes • 192
May Special: The Read-Away Airlines Reading Program • 194
   Preparing the Materials • 195

May Storytimes • 201
May Book Talks • 202
LMC Management • 203
   Computerizing • 203

May Patterns • 205

JUNE

June Calendar • 212
June: A Happy Ending to a Successful Year • 213
If You Have Classes This Month • 213
   June Themes • 213
   June Bulletin Boards • 213
   Corner Ideas • 215

Encouraging Summer Reading • 215
   A Letter to Parents • 215
   Summer Authors Birthday Club • 215
   Introducing the Club • 219

No More Classes—Now What? • 220
   Getting Materials In and Stored • 220
   Inventory, Evaluation, and Weeding • 220
   Checking Audiovisual Equipment • 221
   Ordering Materials • 221
   Thanking Volunteers and Aides • 222

June Patterns • 223

APPENDIX

Eye-Catching Bibliographies (and patterns) • 228
Books to Recommend for Reading Aloud • 228

Sources of Stuffed Animals Based on Book Characters • 235
Sources of Contest Activities • 235
Sources of Inexpensive Prizes • 236
Companies that Provide Book Fairs • 236
Sources of Copyright-Free Clip Art • 237
Sources of Library Skills Games • 238
Sources of Reading Incentive Programs • 239

September

Apples are red,
  fields are gold,
Dandelion heads have
  grown white and old.
The sun is still hot,
  but the nights grow cool;
All nature is saying,
  "It's time for school!"

September Calendar

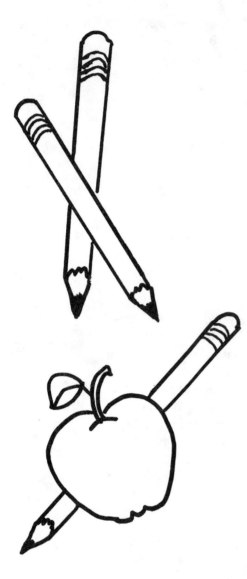

Children's excited voices fill the school halls again and we, too, are excited as we plan for a new year in the library—a year even better than each year before!

First Monday	Labor Day
September 7, 1860	Birthdate of Grandma Moses
September 8	Declaration of Independence published on this day
September 13, 1814	"Star Spangled Banner" written
September 17	Citizenship Day
September 23, 1846	Planet Neptune discovered
September 28, 551 B.C.	Birthdate of Confucious
September 28, 1839	Birthdate of Frances E. Willard

Check your calendar for exact dates of

National Hispanic Heritage Week
Native American Day
First day of autumn

SPECIAL TASKS FOR SEPTEMBER

Returning to the media center after a relaxing summer is both exciting and intimidating. The stacks of magazines and supplier catalogs that have accumulated during the summer are daunting, and the boxes of audiovisual materials and books that need to be opened and processed make you wonder, "Where do I begin?"

Where you begin, of course, depends a lot on how much time you have before the students arrive. If you have the luxury of an extended contract that gives you a week or several days before other teachers arrive, you can begin on the stacks of magazines and unopened boxes. If, however, you have only a day or two before classes begin, you will have to take care of the magazines and boxes later and proceed to bulletin boards, scheduling, room arrangement, and so on.

Let's assume that you have a few days to take care of the accumulated magazines, catalogs, and boxes.

Magazines

Stamp each magazine with the school name on both covers and somewhere in the middle. Skim through the magazines for children quickly to see if there is anything you wish to use, and then place them on the magazine racks. Route professional magazines to teachers or place them in the teachers' room or on a special shelf in the media center. If you have time, skim through the professional magazines and make copies of materials likely to interest particular teachers because of their curriculum or interests. Put these copies in the teachers' mailboxes. If you prefer, put a note on the outside of the magazines, listing pages that might be of interest to the staff.

Catalogs

The catalogs, which seem to accumulate by the dozens, are a never-ending chore. If possible, skim through them as they arrive, marking those you wish to order from and putting them in your "want" file. Those that may be needed at some future date can be filed alphabetically by title. Be sure to throw away last year's catalog from the same company. Catalogs you feel you will never use should be discarded or routed to any teachers who might be interested.

New Materials

When the catalogs and magazines are taken care of, tackle the boxes of new materials. In districts lucky enough to have central processing, all you need to do is check arrivals off your purchase order, shelve them, and file the catalog and shelf cards (or enter them in your computer if your library is computerized). If you do not have a central processing system, you need to check the purchase order with the invoice, marking the items that have arrived. Next, catalog the books and audiovisual materials and prepare either cards and card pockets for each item or put the items in the computer and prepare the books for the computer scanner. In either case, keep a file of completed purchase orders and another for incomplete purchase orders. Check the incomplete purchase orders periodically to make sure that backorders are arriving.

Setting Up Special Areas

Now, at last, it is time to get to the fun part: preparing your room for the coming year. First, look carefully around you to see if it is both usable and attractive. If possible, try to provide the following areas in your facility:

Teaching Area   You will need an area where you can teach skills to the various classes. It should be centrally located, if possible, with either a blackboard or a dry-erase board. You will need several tables with enough chairs to accommodate the largest class you will teach.

Storytime Area   Some libraries have story wells or stages where the children can sit when you read a story to them. If you do not have such an area, try to locate your storytime area in the easy section or in some area away from general traffic. You can make it more inviting by providing some cushions and stuffed animals or book characters.

Nonfiction Area   This should be near the reference section, if possible. A bulletin board near or in this section would be helpful (see "Nonfiction Corner.") There should be one or two tables with chairs in this section.

Fiction Section   This section should have easily accessible shelves and comfortable and inviting chairs, cushions, or even a sofa, if possible.

Easy Section   If you have a separate easy section, the shelves need to be lower, and there should be at least one table with chairs. Stuffed animals on the shelves and on the floor in this section help make it inviting and attractive to younger students.

Card Catalog   Place the card catalog in a central location, but not in the middle of any specific area. If your library is computerized, the computer that students will use should be centrally located.

Reference Section   This should be near the nonfiction area. Put the encyclopedias together and all other reference books on the same subject together on the shelves.

Audiovisual Area Many library and media centers (LMCs) have a section where students may view filmstrips, watch videos, listen to cassettes, use computers, etc. This section must be appealing. If possible, place it in a corner away from the teaching and storytime areas.

Special Interest Corners If possible, provide an authors corner, a nonfiction corner, a contest corner, an arts and crafts corner, and so on. Specific suggestions for these corners are given each month.

Librarian's Station and Work Area Locate this so that you can see most of the library. It should be well lighted and attractive, with posters, seasonal flowers, etc. The book return should be here, in the check-out area if possible.

Games Area Some libraries provide thinking games such as chess, checkers, Mastermind, and so on for children to use during their free time. Some also provide puppets and other imagination-building toys. This area must have cupboards or shelves where the games and toys can be stored, and tables and chairs for students to use when playing the games.

Scheduling Audiovisual Equipment

Scheduling can be a headache, whether it's the scheduling of classes or of audiovisual equipment. You should probably plan the latter first, since many teachers will be anxious to sign up for the equipment. If you have a storage room for your equipment, you might want to put a card pocket and card on each piece of equipment. Keep a chart with pockets for the various types of equipment nearby. When a teacher checks out a movie projector, for example, he or she would write his or her name on the card and then put it in the card pocket for movie projectors. When the projector is returned, the card would be removed and returned to the card pocket on the piece of equipment.

For equipment that is stored in teachers' rooms, you can have a card for each item, have the teachers sign the cards, and then file the cards under the teachers' names. If you have a computerized system, enter the type of equipment and serial number under the teachers' names.

Another method is to keep an audiovisual notebook. Reserve a page for each teacher and record the type of equipment, when it was checked out, and when it was returned.

Yet another way to schedule equipment checked out on a short-term basis is to set up a board with hooks. Above each hook, write the name of each teacher. When the teacher checks out the equipment, he or she hangs the tag for that item on his or her hook. When the teacher returns the item, he or she returns the tag to the item.

Scheduling Classes

There are several books on the subject of scheduling classes. The two main types of scheduling are flexible scheduling and rigid scheduling. The relative merits of each depend on the size of the school, what you are expected to teach, and so on.

You must decide which is better for you. In flexible scheduling, the media center is left unscheduled for large periods of time. The librarian works with the classroom teacher to schedule specific classes for work in certain areas. The librarian must be sure to meet regularly with classroom teachers to ensure that all students are receiving library skills instructions as well as using the library for curriculum purposes. In the best scenario, the skills are taught in connection with curriculum goals.

In rigid scheduling, each class is scheduled into the library for a specific length of time each week. If you use this type of scheduling, try to split in half classes above the second grade so you can teach skills more effectively. It is much easier to help children learn to use the card catalog or find books on the shelves if you have only twelve students instead of twenty-four. Also, you probably don't have enough expensive reference books, such as books of quotations or geographic dictionaries, to use with an entire class. Smaller groups can work in teams with these reference sources.

Whichever method you choose, try to keep your least-scheduled days on Monday and Friday because these are the days most often lost to holidays, conferences, and so on. This will give you fewer classes to make up when those special days disrupt your schedule. Try to plan your schedule with each teacher. It is a good idea to have your schedule ready before the beginning of school; teachers appreciate being able to bring their classes into the library as soon as possible.

Preparing an Overall Plan for the Year

An overall plan for your library program will help you in the coming months as your schedule becomes full and there is little time for planning. It need not be complex or complete, just an outline providing a framework to build on. Take time now to choose a theme for each month and to choose the library skills on which you will focus in each month for each grade. (Theme ideas are listed for each month in each chapter of this book.) When the specific month is near, fit the bulletin boards, the various special corners, the storytimes, contests, and, if possible, library skills lessons into this central theme. Forms are provided for both your overall yearly plan and your monthly plan.

Once you have planned your year in this broad fashion, you are ready to prepare for the current month, September.

———————— SEPTEMBER THEMES ————————

Some ideas for a central theme for September include *Schools—Then and Now, Off to a Great Start, Getting to Know You,* and *Old Book Friends Welcome You Back.* Before you choose one of these themes or one of your own, read over the activities and ideas that follow to see which theme might fit best with your available materials and your own style of teaching.

AN OVERALL PLAN FOR THE LIBRARY AND MEDIA CENTER FOR THE YEAR _____

MONTH	THEME	SKILLS TO BE EMPHASIZED
September		
October		
November		
December		
January		
February		
March		
April		
May		
June		

PLAN FOR THE MONTH OF _____

Theme

Authors Birthday Club

Contest Corner

Arts and Crafts Corner

Nonfiction Corner

Skills to be covered

Grade

Grade

Grade

Grade

Grade

Storytimes/Book Talks

Bulletin Boards

Notes

If you have other ideas for September themes, take time to jot them down below so you won't forget them.

OTHER SEPTEMBER THEMES: _____

_____

_____

_____

SPECIAL DAYS IN SEPTEMBER

If you chose *Schools—Then and Now* as your theme, you may want to see if the school would enjoy participating in a "Back to the School of the Past" day. On the designated day, teachers, students, secretaries (you may have to exclude both secretaries and cooks because of the nature of their work), and teacher aides will use nothing that was not available before the year 1900. Of course, there will be no computers in use that day, and microwave ovens will not be available in the staff room. If you really want to get into the spirit of the day, students and staff could dress in pre-1900 costumes and bring a bag lunch instead of having hot food in the cafeteria. Teachers would have to write their lessons on the blackboard or instruct students orally. Naturally, there will be no movies, videos, or other audiovisual instruction. This activity is fun and makes everyone appreciate the many tools we have available today. For the library, a display of old books compared with new ones is appropriate.

If you can find some older person who would be willing to come and talk to the students beforehand to tell them about the schools of the past from their own personal experience, the day would be even more meaningful. Students find it difficult to realize that even something as simple as a ballpoint pen was not available. The older students can help decide what was or was not available by using *Famous First Facts* (a good way to introduce this interesting reference source).

An activity that goes well with the theme *Old Book Friends Welcome You Back* has students draw their favorite book character and on a day specified as "Old Friends Day" bring them to the library for display.

OTHER SPECIAL DAY IDEAS: _____

_____

_____

_____

_____

SEPTEMBER BULLETIN BOARDS

Both bulletin board ideas for September emphasize reading. "Look Who's Reading" shows children that reading for fun is something everyone can enjoy. Take pictures of students, teachers, the principal, cook, and custodians while they are reading. Mount the pictures on bright-colored books (a pattern is provided at the end of this chapter) and print the title of that person's favorite book under each photo.

"I Wish I Could Read!" features a bewildered caveman who cannot tell which direction he should travel because he cannot read. A bright blue background with a brown ground and green plants would be appropriate. Additional words saying, "Aren't you glad YOU can?" could be added if desired. Patterns for both bulletin boards are provided at the end of this chapter.

OTHER BULLETIN BOARD IDEAS: _____

_____

_____

_____

_____ *SEPTEMBER AUTHORS* _____ *BIRTHDAY CLUB*

Since this is the first month of the school year, plan on explaining to each group of students, when they arrive for orientation, that they can become a member of the author birthday club by reading at least three books by any one of the authors. (You may prefer to choose another number, depending on the author. Three of Roald Dahl's books, for example, would take a great deal longer than three of Tomie dePaola's.) Or, you may want students to read a certain number of books by *different* September authors.

Get students enthusiastic about the authors by giving brief book talks about them or reading their books during storytimes. Explain that those children who do the reading required will be invited to a birthday party at the end of September. This is a good time to decide whether you are going to bake the monthly birthday cake or would like to see if the parent-teacher organization might undertake a cake a month after you explain to them how it will encourage reading. If you want to have them do it, contact them early and get a schedule of which parent is to be responsible for the cake each month. Then be sure to call the parent a couple of days before the cake needs to arrive to remind him or her.

You may want to put the names of the students who have read the required number of books on the bulletin board as they complete the books, or you may prefer to put them on the October authors birthday bulletin board.

A form on which students can record their reading is included. (There are two to each page; copy and then cut them apart.) As students turn in these forms, keep them in a folder, and two or three days before the end of the month, make out invitations to all who have completed the requirement.

At the party, you can ask children to sit in a circle and tell the group which book was their favorite. If possible, take pictures of the group to post on the bulletin board. Let them enjoy the cake, and if you have time, show them a just-for-fun movie or video—one about any of the September authors' books would be especially nice. As the students leave, try to give each a button saying something about reading, or a special button you can make that says "I'm an Authors Club Member." (A pattern for two of these is provided.) If buttons are too expensive, try bookmarks.

The authors born in September are a particularly prolific group, with most of them having many well-loved books to their credit. For this month's bulletin board, choose just those you wish to feature, or use all of them. If you choose just a few, you can print the name of each author on one of the candles you put on the birthday cake.

September Authors

September 3, 1906	Aileen Fisher
September 3, 1929	Aliki
September 4, 1924	Joan Aiken
September 4, 1912	Syd Hoff
September 6, 1917	Frank Modell
September 8, 1940	Jack Prelutsky
September 11, 1926	Alfred Slote
September 11, 1946	Anthony Browne
September 13, 1916	Roald Dahl
September 15, 1934	Tomie DePaola
September 16, 1898	H. A. Rey
September 20, 1928	Donald Hall
September 24, 1932	Jane Louise Curry
September 24, 1913	Wilson Rawls
September 27, 1933	Paul Goble
September 29, 1923	Stan Berenstain

_____

_____

_____

_____

_____

_____

_____

(Student's Name)

_____

(Grade)

YOU ARE INVITED to the
AUTHORS BIRTHDAY PARTY

for the month of _____.

Date: _____

Time: _____

_____

(LIBRARIAN)

- -

SAMPLE PATTERNS
FOR AUTHORS BIRTHDAY CLUB BUTTONS, BOOKMARK

AUTHORS
BIRTHDAY

CLUB
MEMBER

I
LOVE
BOOKS!

AUTHORS BIRTHDAY CLUB MEMBER

STUDENT RECORD SHEET FOR

_____ **AUTHORS BIRTHDAY CLUB**
(Month)

NAME OF AUTHOR: _____

TITLE OF BOOK: _____

NAME OF AUTHOR: _____

TITLE OF BOOK: _____

NAME OF AUTHOR: _____

TITLE OF BOOK: _____

_____ HAS READ THE BOOKS LISTED ABOVE.

_____
(SIGNATURE OF PARENT OR GUARDIAN)

STUDENT RECORD SHEET FOR

_____ **AUTHORS BIRTHDAY CLUB**
(Month)

NAME OF AUTHOR: _____

TITLE OF BOOK: _____

NAME OF AUTHOR: _____

TITLE OF BOOK: _____

NAME OF AUTHOR: _____

TITLE OF BOOK: _____

_____ HAS READ THE BOOKS LISTED ABOVE.

_____
(SIGNATURE OF PARENT OR GUARDIAN)

If you use many authors, it would be better to print their names and birthdates on colorful red apples and brightly colored pencils that can be placed around the cake. Make the large birthday cake out of construction paper, using the pattern provided at the end of this chapter (or one of your own) and mount it on the bulletin board that will be your authors birthday corner for the year. Make large letters that say, "HAPPY BIRTHDAY TO SEPTEMBER AUTHORS." Put a table or low bookcase under or near the bulletin board and display books by the chosen authors on it.

Some other ideas: You or a student can write to each featured author in care of his or her publisher, explaining that he or she is to be featured in your authors corner and requesting that he or she write a letter to the students in your school. (A sample letter is provided.)

Let students research a featured author in place of one of the book requirements. Their reports on the author could be posted on or near the authors corner.

OTHER IDEAS: _____

_____

_____

_____

_____

_____

_____

SAMPLE LETTER TO AN AUTHOR
FOR THE AUTHORS CORNER

Memorial School Library   (Or use letterhead)
1 Second Street
Anytown, OR 99999

September 10, 1992

Dear _____AUTHOR_____:

Since your birthday is in the month of _____MONTH_____ and you are one of the
students' favorite authors, we plan to feature you as one of the authors in our library's
Authors Corner.

We wonder if you could please find the time to write a brief letter or note to the
students of our school? It would please them very much to see something from you
featured in our Authors Corner along with copies of your books.

The students read many of your books, but they seem to particularly enjoy
_____TITLE_____.

Thank you for writing books our students enjoy!

Sincerely,

_____YOUR NAME_____
Library Media Specialist
Memorial School Library

Enclosure
(BE SURE TO INCLUDE A SELF-ADDRESSED, STAMPED ENVELOPE!)

SEPTEMBER CONTEST
CORNER

Many students will use and appreciate a corner in which each month they can find interesting, enjoyable, but educational contests. You will find that many enter the easy contests, but there are always some who enjoy a challenge and will try more difficult contests. If possible, have several types of contests in this corner so all ages can participate and different interests can be matched.

Appropriate for September (and fitting nicely into an overall theme of *Getting to Know You*) is a contest that requires a picture of each teacher. Arrange these on a bulletin board with each teacher's name beneath his or her picture. On small, cut-out strips of paper or in a list, write something interesting about each teacher (teachers will need to supply both this and the photo). Students must match the teacher with the interesting fact. Example: "I went to Europe this summer," or "My favorite recreation is playing golf." Students who enter this contest must ask teachers questions before and after school but not during classes. Teachers will be instructed to answer honestly but not to volunteer information in their classes. Students and teachers alike usually enjoy this activity, and it helps the students get to know the teachers.

Make the letters for the caption large and colorful. Mount each teacher's photo on a colorful piece of construction paper and the interesting facts on another color of paper. If you have a small faculty, it would be nice to include secretaries, aides, custodians, and cooks.

Set the deadline for entry in the contests for several days before the end of the month so you can award the prizes and post the winners before the new month's contests.

Another good contest for September asks students to match characters with books. It would fit in well with the overall theme of *Old Book Friends Welcome You Back.* Write book titles on a book shape (provided at the end of this chapter). Then put characters from each book on the bulletin board. If you are lucky, you can find pictures of these in catalogs, magazines, or book jackets. An attractive alternative is to cut out silhouettes of boys and girls and put the name of the character under each figure. (Silhouette patterns are provided.) You can have students match book titles to characters, or just put characters on the bulletin board and have them come up with the title of one book where this character can be found. An appropriate caption is "Do You Know These Book Friends?"

A contest which would fit in well with an overall theme of *Off to a Great Start* begins with providing maps of your library. A simple line drawing is best. Under the map, write the names of the different areas in the library, giving a number to each. The students can then explore the library and put the correct number of each area in the proper place on the map. (If you prefer, this activity can be done in your initial orientation classes.) Since this is one of those activities that require only minimal effort, many children will probably enter—so if you plan to award prizes, make the prize small, perhaps a bookmark or sticker.

Don't forget that many activities available in teacher magazines and library media resource books* can make excellent contests that require minimal preparation. You will find ready-to-use crossword puzzles, research contests, and other activities already keyed into the month.

Not everyone feels comfortable awarding prizes, but you will find that there is more participation in the contests if you recognize the winners in some way. Having

---

*Such as *Reading Bingos,* © 1989 by The Center for Applied Research in Education.

them come to the library at a certain time to get their prizes and posting pictures of the prize winners on the bulletin board helps to publicize the contest corner. Some children enjoy doing the contests whether there is a prize or not, and you will find many participating even though the prizes are small.

Prizes can be gift books from various book clubs, bookmarks purchased from library supply catalogs, small prizes you can find at garage sales, or small carnival-type prizes found in various carnival supply catalogs. A list of these catalogs is included in the Appendix.

OTHER CONTEST IDEAS: _____

_____

_____

_____

_____

SEPTEMBER ARTS AND CRAFTS CORNER

Since this is the first month of the school year, you may not be familiar with any students who might be gifted in art and could be featured in your arts and crafts corner. Instead, you might feature any new arts and crafts books you have recently purchased. Promote them by making a few items to display in the corner along with the books containing the directions or suggestions. In early classes, exhibit some of the books and mention some of the projects that can be found in them.

If you wish to feature just one type of book each month, September is a good time to feature books that provide nature crafts (such as seed pictures, pressed flower crafts, etc.) and drawing books that focus on scenery or landscapes.

If you have room, try to feature an artist each month. Van Gogh is good for September because his "Sunflowers" and paintings of wheat fields are so appropriate for the season. Post his self-portrait with a little biographical sketch beside it, or challenge students to answer some questions about Van Gogh by using the encyclopedia or other reference source. Sample questions are as follows:

- Where was Van Gogh born?
  (Groot-zundert, The Netherlands)
- Look at several prints of paintings by Van Gogh and tell which one you like best and why.
  (varies)
- Did Van Gogh receive recognition and wealth for his paintings?
  (no)

Try to have no more than three or four questions about the month's featured artist, since more will discourage some who might otherwise do a little research.

During the month, encourage students to exhibit in this corner any artwork or craft they have made from suggestions in a book. Some may be willing to come to the library before or after school or during recess to show other students how to do a craft. Origami is one craft some students are good at and can demonstrate to others.

Near the end of the month, take a picture of any student who has demonstrated or exhibited in your arts and crafts corner. You can post these pictures or start a scrapbook of school artists and craftspeople. Teachers and other staff members should also be encouraged to exhibit or demonstrate any art or craft at which they are proficient.

OTHER ARTS AND CRAFTS IDEAS: _____

_____

_____

_____

_____

SEPTEMBER NONFICTION CORNER

Feature a special kind of nonfiction book each month. September is a good time to feature those about autumn sports, such as football, soccer, and baseball (especially the World Series), and Olympic books (if it's an Olympic year).

Another possibility: Feature a display of old and modern textbooks. If you can find some, also display both old and new general nonfiction books. Students will be surprised at the color and excitement of new books compared to what was available in the past. This display would fit in with a *Schools Then and Now* theme. If you have a bulletin board near this corner, make a large caption: "Books: Then and Now!" If you have old book jackets available, arrange a display with newer jackets; if not, set up a display of books under the bulletin board. You can also have students answer questions about the books, such as

- Which book is the oldest? (Check the copyright date.)
- Which book is the newest?
- Which is the oldest copyrighted book to have color illustrations?

Whether this is done as a voluntary, contest-like activity or as a requirement in a skills class, caution the children to use great care in handling the old books. (If you don't have any old books, ask the faculty to bring some in. Some classrooms will have old textbooks stowed away.)

You may want to feature a research question of the week in this corner. Sample questions for September could be

- What is the autumnal equinox and when does it occur?
  (end of summer, beginning of autumn; September 21)
- Agatha Christie was born in September. Who is she?
  (famous English mystery writer)
- Where was the first public school in the United States?
  (Boston, Massachusetts)
- According to the latest almanac, how many children are there in public elementary schools in the United States?
  (varies)

At the end of each week, post the correct answer and the names of any students who answered the questions correctly. You can keep a record of who answers the questions and award a prize when a student has correctly answered ten weekly questions (or any number you feel appropriate) and invite the student to become a member of a research club. Or, if you prefer, you could just post the names and award a small prize such as a bookmark or sticker.

OTHER NONFICTION CORNER IDEAS: _____

_____

_____

_____

_____

_____ *SEPTEMBER SKILLS CLASSES* _____

Orientation Classes

Since you will be very busy the first week of school unpacking boxes, preparing displays of new books, and so on, it is better not to begin the full library schedule the first week. Instead, let each teacher sign up for a time to bring his or her class into the library for a brief orientation. Ask the teacher to remain with his or her class for this first time at least, so the teacher may also learn the library procedures the students will be asked to follow. It also helps you if the teachers know about the various corners, contests, and so on, so they can participate and encourage their students to participate.

For primary grades, plan to escort the children briefly around the library while you explain the different areas in greater or lesser detail depending on the students. Kindergarten teachers may prefer to wait a week or several weeks before bringing their classes, so the children may become accustomed to school before having yet another new experience. Whenever they do come in, show them just the easy section at first and have many books displayed for them to choose from. Later, after they have become adept at choosing books for themselves in this section, show them the nonfiction section and the audiovisual check-out sections.

First graders who have attended kindergarten will already be familiar with check-out procedures and with the easy, nonfiction, and audiovisual sections. You might show them one of the corners, such as the arts and crafts corner, but save the other corners for another time. Review your procedures for check-out, how many books they are allowed to check out, and how long they may keep the books. With all primary students, save time for a story before they return to their classrooms.

In orientation classes with older children, include check-out procedures and different areas of the library just as you did with the primary students, but also emphasize each of the corners and encourage participation in them. If you have time, you might do a book talk about one or more of the books in the nonfiction corner or give students time to try one of the contests in the contest corner.

Other Skills Classes

You have already designed your overall skills plan for the year, so now is the time to plan specifically for the skills classes. Students learn more and enjoy it more if they get to practice new skills. For example, if you are teaching location skills to second, third, or fourth graders, give the children call numbers on cards and let them go to the shelves and locate the books, rather than giving them worksheet pages for seat work. For September, try using a book shape for cards (you can use the pattern for the "Do You Know These Book Friends?" contest, provided at the end of this chapter). Put a different call number and book title on enough cards so that each member of the class can be given one. Spread out the call numbers in different areas of the section to prevent students from pushing and shoving to find their books. For example, if you are teaching how to locate books in the easy section, make call numbers and titles using widely spaced authors such as Harry Allard, Marc Brown, Tomie dePaola, Dr. Seuss, Bernard Waber, etc.

Name _____   Date _____

SEPTEMBER SCAVENGER HUNT

How well do you know your library? See if you can find each of the following items. Remember that you may not run, but go as quickly as you can and then return this sheet to the librarian.

1. Find a book in the fiction section that has a color in its title: _____

2. Find a book in the easy section that has a call number $\overset{\text{E}}{\text{St.}}$ Write its title here: _____
   _____

3. From the card catalog, write the heading of one of the dividers in any drawer you choose:
   _____

4. From the nonfiction section of the library, write the title of any book in the **808.7** section:
   _____

5. Go to the reference section and write the name of any encyclopedia set available there:
   _____

6. What is the name of your library's unabridged dictionary?
   _____

7. What is the librarian's name? (Spell it correctly!)
   _____

8. What is the name of the library aide? (Spell it correctly, too!)
   _____

9. In the card catalog, find the title of any audiovisual item and write it here: _____
   _____. What kind of audiovisual item is it? (video, filmstrip, cassette,
   etc.) _____

10. What is the name of one reference book that is not an encyclopedia, dictionary, or
    almanac? _____

This activity is a great favorite with second and third graders, so plan on making enough cards so some students can find more than one book. Make cards for all sections of the library. Second and third graders might begin with only the easy section call numbers and later in the year use the fiction section cards. Fourth graders can begin on mixed cards of easy or fiction and later in the year move to cards from the nonfiction section; fifth and sixth graders can probably begin the year with call numbers from all sections. (Some groups may need to review the nonfiction sections before using those call numbers.)

In an early class for grades four and up, you might have a scavenger hunt where students in pairs (this reduces congestion) find things in different sections of the library. A sample instruction sheet is included; modify it to suit your particular situation. This is a good activity no matter what your theme, but it fits particularly well with *Getting to Know You.* Playing library skills games is a good way for students to learn skills painlessly, so try to use games as a skills activity at least once a month. Games teaching card catalog, reference skills, library terms, etc. are available from a variety of companies (a list is included in the Appendix).

If, for each month, you plan one session of book talks or audiovisual presentation of books, one session of library skills games, one session of active practice of skills, and one session of an interesting type of research activity, you will find students enjoying their visits to the library.

Management Tip: If you live near a book jobber, the first week of school might be a good time for you to visit and choose books for purchase. If so, remember to schedule the orientation classes so one day remains free for the visit.

OTHER LIBRARY SKILLS IDEAS: _____

_____

_____

_____

_____

_____ SEPTEMBER STORYTIMES _____

Naturally, you'll want to choose especially interesting stories for your first month of storytimes. Just a few of the many possible titles are listed here.

Monkey Face, by Frank Asch. This book is great for first storytime for kindergarten because it shows a loving connection with home and has the repetition and humor that young children love.

The Monkey and the Crocodile, by Paul Galdone. This is one young children also enjoy, because the wily monkey outwits the ravenous crocodile.

Fat Cat, by Jack Kent. This is another book that kindergarteners particularly enjoy.

Miss Nelson Has a Field Day, by Harry Allard. If students haven't already been overexposed to this book, it's a great one for second and third grade. It's about a bad football team and how Miss Nelson shapes them up—appropriate at this time of year.

The Day the Teacher Went Bananas, by James Howe. Students were surprised to find their teacher was a gorilla. This book fits in well with a back-to-school theme and is suitable for most primary grades.

Rolling Harvey Down the Hill, by Jack Prelutsky. This is a good book to use to hook third graders on poetry books. They will all want to borrow this one, but you can interest them in similar books by Prelutsky and Shel Silverstein.

Annie Bananie, by Leah Komaiko. This is a good one to use with first or second graders who may have had to move from one school to another and leave a best friend behind.

As part of the theme of *Old Book Friends Welcome You Back,* remember to read old favorites such as "Goldilocks and the Three Bears," "Three Little Pigs," and more. Classic folk tales and fairy tales are good for older primary students.

OTHER TITLES YOU LIKE: _____

_____

_____

_____

_____

_____

_____

_____

_____

_____

Management Tip: In September, it is a good idea to set up a method to keep track of the books you read to each class. After several years of reading and telling stories and giving book talks, you will find it difficult to remember if you have read a particular book to a certain grade.

Try keeping a file card on each book you read. File the cards by grade level, and you can quickly see which books you have already read to the class and which are still available. The card system also allows you to add new books quickly and delete others. It may be time-consuming when you first set up your file, but it will save you time later.

Keep a similar file card for book talks. Mark the grade level at the top of each card. Holiday stories can be designated by a colored line (orange for Halloween, green for Christmas, etc.) or a pictorial symbol.

		K
ARTHUR'S NOSE by Marc Brown		
year	class read to	date read
1991-92	*1-B and 1-C*	*Sept. 22*
1992-93	*1-B and 1-W*	*Feb. 2*
1993-94		
1994-95		
1995-96		

SEPTEMBER BOOK TALKS

In keeping with a *Back to School* or *Schools—Then and Now* theme, here are some books about kids and schools that you might like to use for book talks with your fourth, fifth, and sixth grades.

13 Ways to Sink a Sub, by Jamie Gilson. The kids in the fourth-grade class play a game. Whenever they have a substitute teacher, the boys and girls vie to see who can make the substitute cry. If you don't wish to use this one, you might recommend it to teachers, since some talks about courteous behavior with substitutes could follow.

The Iceberg and Its Shadow, by Sheila Greenburg. This book is probably best for fifth or sixth graders because it tells how a new student disrupts the friendships in a sixth-grade classroom. It is also good for discussion.

Ramona the Pest, by Beverly Cleary. Fourth-grade students are old enough to understand and get a laugh from the antics of Ramona in kindergarten, who sat in her seat waiting for a gift because her teacher told her to "sit here for the present." This book is also good because when the whole class wants to check it out after you tell about it, there are many other Ramona books to offer them.

Nothing's Fair in Fifth Grade, by Barthe DeClements. This book is about a girl who is made fun of and shunned by the class because of her immense size. As the story develops, the students begin to sympathize with her and try to help her in school and with her seemingly uncaring mother.

Other titles which are useful and in a lighter vein include *The Great Brain at the Academy,* by John Fitzgerald; *Soup for President,* by Robert Peck; and *Nutty for President,* by Dean Hughes.

OTHER TITLES YOU LIKE: _____

_____

_____

_____

_____

_____

_____

_____

_____

_____ *LMC MANAGEMENT* _____

Volunteers can be the extra help you need to accomplish all the teaching and planning expected of you in the modern LMC. Both parent volunteers and student volunteers can contribute greatly to your program.

Parent Volunteers

Parent volunteers can free you and your library aide to have more time available to plan for and work with students. They can card and shelve books as well as work at the check-out desk. They can cut letters for bulletin boards and take bulletin boards down. Some volunteers are artistic and enjoy making the bulletin boards. Others like to type and can type requests for free materials for you or write to chambers of commerce or other places for free information. Occasionally, a mother or father librarian volunteers and can file cards and do other tasks of a librarian. Their help is invaluable, and you will usually find them to be dependable.

Be sure to thank your volunteers each time they come and to praise them for what they do well. A small gift or a tea at the end of the year is also nice, since it shows them how much you appreciate them.

A form is provided here for inviting parents to be volunteers and also to express your appreciation.

Student Volunteers

Students from grade four up make excellent library aides. Fifth graders, in particular, can be helpful because they are knowledgeable about carding, shelving, and so on, and they are often enthusiastic about helping.

Sometime during September, send invitation sign-up sheets to classes in the grades you have chosen for your student aides. (Naturally, you will want to enlist the involved teachers' support beforehand.) After interested students have signed

SAMPLE PARENT-VOLUNTEER LETTER

SCHOOL NAME
SCHOOL ADDRESS
CITY AND TOWN

DATE

DEAR _____:

Thank you for volunteering to work in the _____ School Library. The parent volunteers help to make our library an enjoyable place for our students.

There are many different things you could do to help us. We would like to know which you would most enjoy doing and if you have a particular skill or talent that you would like to share with our school. Please check the activities you're interested in on the following list and then add anything that you would like to share with the students.

_____ SHELVE BOOKS

_____ WORK AT THE CHECK-OUT DESK

_____ WORK WITH SMALL GROUPS OF CHILDREN DOING VARIOUS TASKS

_____ HELP AT THE ARTS AND CRAFTS CORNER SHOWING STUDENTS HOW TO DO A CRAFT

_____ TYPE CARDS AND OTHER LIBRARY MATERIALS

_____ REPAIR BOOKS

_____ PREPARE OR HELP PREPARE BULLETIN BOARDS

_____ KEEP THE LIBRARY OPEN DURING THE LIBRARIAN'S LUNCH TIME

_____ LAMINATE MATERIALS FOR TEACHERS

_____ OTHER: _____

_____

What time would be best for you to work? _____

Again, thank you very much. We will be contacting you to arrange a time that is best for you.

Sincerely,

_____, Librarian

their names, find a time when they can all come to the library to meet with you and learn their duties, when their appointed time will be, and so on. If you feel the students need to know more about what you plan to ask them to do, tell them about your plan in one of the first library skills or check-out classes and give them the opportunity to sign up at that time.

At the organizational meeting, explain the duties of the student aides. Students are capable of shelving (you may wish to reserve nonfiction shelving until later in the year when you are sure they know the system), carding, writing overdue notes, cutting out bulletin board materials, running errands, and working at the check-out desk. Most students prefer the latter to all other tasks, so it's a good idea to have some sort of system for moving each aide to a different job each week. Make aides aware of this so they will not beg you for a preferred job. One relatively easy system: Make a small cardboard sheet for each day of the week. Put four card pockets on each board and mark them Desk, Carding, Shelving, and Various Duties (or whatever other jobs you have decided on). Then put each aide's name on a cardboard strip and assign him or her a day of the week and a time for working. If you have different times during the day, use a different color of cardboard for each; for example, all children who work before school could have their names printed on yellow cardboard, those who work at noon on red, and those who work after school on green. That way, you can see at a glance which student should be working and you can use the same pockets for all shifts in a day. Each Monday, you or your aide can move the students' names one pocket to the right, so each week they will have a different job.

Since aides will be expected to be dependable about coming to work, you need some kind of a system to monitor this. It is simple, and the students seem to enjoy it, so let each one put a star on his or her name card when finished with work each week. It will be easy to see if some are missing their assigned time.

At your first meeting with the new aides, explain how you will monitor their work performance. Tell them that they are to come in at their assigned time, look at their day's assignment card, and see where their name is. That is their job for the day. They must do each job well, not just one favored job. Let them know your expectations for attendance. For example, you may say that they may have two or three unexcused absences during the year, but if they have more their names will be removed from your list of aides. Explain that this is necessary because you depend on them and have jobs for them that will not get done if they do not show up.

This first meeting is a great time to show a video or slide show of student aides working in the library. (During the year, take some videos or slides of students doing their jobs so you can show this to new aides the following year.) Or, you could have one or two of your best student aides from the previous year come to this meeting and explain to the new aides about their jobs. If this is your first year using student aides, of course, you will just have to tell them about their jobs and how to do them.

It is nice to provide buttons for the aides to wear when they work, designating them as student library aides. These are not necessary, of course, but something special that students appreciate. These buttons are available from various library supply companies, or you can make them yourself.

During the year, it is a good idea to have two or three meetings with your aides, helping them or telling them how much you appreciate their help. A video and treats are nice extras. Remembering them at Halloween, Christmas, and Valentine's Day is also appreciated. At the end of the year, in the school's recognition assembly, honor your student aides by presenting them each with a library aide certificate (provided).

FORMS TO USE IN THE STUDENT AIDE PROGRAM

- -

Thank you for volunteering to be a student library aide! Your scheduled time to help in the library is at _____ on every _____.

We will be counting on your help, so please try to be there at your scheduled time.

_____
LIBRARIAN

- -

CALLING ALL LIBRARY AIDES!

Please come to the library for an

Appreciation Party!

We appreciate all your help during the year, and we would like to honor you with a party!

Please come on _____ at _____.

_____
LIBRARIAN

- -

To: _____

According to our records, you have not been coming to the library to work as an aide during your scheduled time. If you still wish to be a library aide, please come and see me. If you no longer wish to serve as a library aide, we will remove your name from our list of helpers.

Thank you.

_____
LIBRARIAN

THIS CERTIFICATE IS AWARDED TO

_____

who served as

Library Aide

in _____ SCHOOL

DURING THE _____ SCHOOL YEAR

_____ LIBRARIAN

PATTERNS

October

All of nature puts on a show
In October's bright blue weather:
The hills, the trees a golden glow,
Each leaf a scarlet feather.

October Calendar

By the beginning of October, the students and teachers have settled down to the new school year. Autumn is in the air, and the children's eyes begin to gleam with thoughts of Halloween and the other holidays to follow. This is a month with so many events on which to focus (World Series, football games, Columbus Day, autumn weather, Halloween, etc.) that it is relatively easy to plan and prepare bulletin boards, corner activities, and skills activities. It is a month to enjoy for both teachers and students.

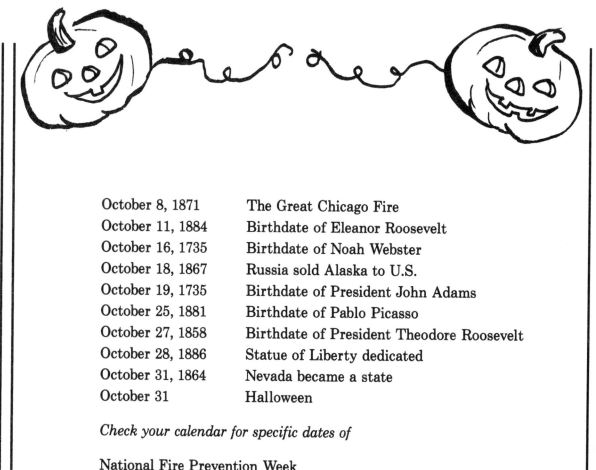

October 8, 1871	The Great Chicago Fire
October 11, 1884	Birthdate of Eleanor Roosevelt
October 16, 1735	Birthdate of Noah Webster
October 18, 1867	Russia sold Alaska to U.S.
October 19, 1735	Birthdate of President John Adams
October 25, 1881	Birthdate of Pablo Picasso
October 27, 1858	Birthdate of President Theodore Roosevelt
October 28, 1886	Statue of Liberty dedicated
October 31, 1864	Nevada became a state
October 31	Halloween

Check your calendar for specific dates of

National Fire Prevention Week
Canadian Thanksgiving Day
Columbus Day

_____ *OCTOBER THEMES* _____

Halloween lends itself to storytimes and book talks since there are so many books published that fit in this category. *I Love a Mystery* is one possible theme. Feature mysteries on bulletin boards and in book talks and storytimes. To accompany this theme, you might have a mystery box each week, with one new clue posted each day. The first student to guess the contents of the box would win a small prize. For example, if you have a toy spider in the box, you can use these clues:

- Clue 1: An animal is in the box.
- Clue 2: This animal can be found all over the world.
- Clue 3: This animal is very small but is a carnivore.
- Clue 4: This animal is found both indoors and outdoors.
- Clue 5: This animal is an arachnid.

By clue 5, any student with the ambition to look in a dictionary will know the answer. Other appropriate possibilities for the box include a pumpkin seed, a candle, a dictionary or thesaurus, or a small teddy bear.

Other mystery ideas: Place a pumpkin on the check-out desk and make a face on it with felt-tip pens. Place a sign next to it that says, "It's really quite a mystery! Guess how many seeds in me?" Let students guess, and near the end of the month have your student aides count the seeds and declare a winner. Another idea is to wrap a mystery book in brown paper. Give clues each day until someone guesses which book it is. For example,

- Clue 1: It is a fiction book.
- Clue 2: The author is Jamie Gilson.
- Clue 3: Its copyright date is _____.
- Clue 4: It has _____ number of pages.
- Clue 5: The title has _____ number of words.

This should send some students to the card catalog!

Other theme ideas: *Teddy Bears, Teddy Bears,* and *English—What a Strange Language!* (the latter allows you to feature books such as *The King Who Reigned,* by Fred Gwynne, or other books featuring idioms).

OTHER IDEAS FOR THEMES: _____

_____

_____

_____

_____

———————— *SPECIAL DAYS IN OCTOBER* ————————

Dictionary Day

In honor of the birthday of Noah Webster, born October 16, 1758, it might be fun to declare this date a Dictionary Day or Dictionary Week. Have skills classes practice dictionary skills. Have a Word for the Day (or if you choose Dictionary Week, one for each day of the week) and give an immediate small award to each student who correctly uses the word in a sentence spoken to you.

Other activities: Remind students of the many types of dictionaries—rhyming, crossword puzzle, thesaurus, foreign language, etc. Challenge a class or an enrichment group to compile their own dictionary, such as a dictionary of slang used by the students, or a dictionary of favorite leisure-time activities. Remind students that all dictionaries are in alphabetical order and that there should be more than one entry per letter (if there is only one entry per letter, it is more of an alphabet book).

Teddy Bear Day

October 27 is the birthday of Teddy Roosevelt, for whom the Teddy Bear is supposedly named. This makes the day an appropriate one in which to celebrate Teddy Bear Day. On this day, let any child who wishes to do so display his or her teddy bear in the LMC. Put a label on each teddy bear so all will know who brought the bear.

Feature books about bears during the week by displaying them and by reading them during storytime. Be sure to include Paddington, Winnie-the-Pooh, Gentle Ben, and newer bears like the Care Bears, Little Bear by Minarik, and Little Bear by Janice. New books about teddy bears are published often, so include any you have bought recently.

If your students enjoy contests, you could award a prize ribbon or button for the biggest teddy bear, the smallest, the most loved (probably the most tattered), the oldest, the newest, and so on. You can probably come up with a ribbon for each. If you prefer, just give a gummi bear or similar small treat to each exhibitor.

See if anyone can use their research skills to find out when the first teddy bear was made. You might also have a student (or two or three) research Teddy Roosevelt and report on him to different groups.

Most communities have people who collect teddy bears and who are willing and sometimes delighted to come and talk to the students about their collection. Try to get someone who is comfortable talking to students and who will not talk above their heads. Ask a student to be responsible for introducing this speaker and another to be responsible for thanking the speaker. Still another might write a thank-you letter. If the speaker is to address all the students, ask students to bring their teddy bears to the assembly. It might be better if they lined up their bears behind the speaker so they won't be able to play with them while the speaker is talking. If there's time, each student who brought a bear can come forward and show his or her bear and tell its name and something interesting about it.

TEDDY BEAR TAGS FOR TEDDY BEAR DAY

Students usually enjoy Teddy Bear Day, and it makes a nice change in the middle of Halloween activities.

OTHER SPECIAL DAY IDEAS: _____

_____

_____

_____

_____

OCTOBER BULLETIN BOARDS

October bulletin boards offer many opportunities for colorful, interesting displays. There are so many Halloween books available that there is an abundance of book jackets you can feature. The two bulletin boards featured this month are "Good Reading for October" and "Whooo Do You Know?" The "Good Reading for October" board displays colorful book jackets highlighted by two black cats sporting colorful bows. Cut the cats from black construction paper after enlarging them to whatever size fits best. Cut the cats' eyes from green construction paper and use pink for the nose. Outline the mouth and whiskers in white (try white tempera or white correction fluid). Cut the cats' bowties from orange paper and draw black or white polka dots on them. Feature book jackets for Halloween.

The "Whooo Do You Know?" bulletin board features book jackets from biographies. Include one for Columbus, Theodore Roosevelt, Eleanor Roosevelt, and

President John Adams, if available, since their birthdays are in October. Or feature the book jackets from some of the newest biographies in your collection. The owls can be cut from tan paper, with the wings, tail, and ear sections colored or outlined in dark brown felt-tip pen. The eyes can be cut from either yellow or orange paper. A dark blue background would be colorful. Cut the letters from black or yellow construction paper, or use point-back plastic letters. Patterns for both bulletin boards are at the end of this chapter.

OCTOBER AUTHORS BIRTHDAY CLUB

If you had an Authors Birthday Club party in September, there will probably be many students who are excited about reading in October's birthday club activity. Introduce the October authors during storytimes, book talks, and skills sessions. Explain the procedure and show the confirmation notes students must return from their parents (see September).

The bulletin board for the Authors Birthday Club this month can be colorful. Put the featured authors' names on bright orange pumpkins. Surround the birthday cake with these colorful pumpkins, and cut letters or use point-back letters to spell the caption, "HAPPY BIRTHDAY TO OCTOBER AUTHORS!" A pumpkin pattern can be found at the end of this chapter.

It is usually wise to feature at least three authors who write picture books and three who write for third- through sixth-grade readers. If you feature fewer, you may find you do not have enough books to satisfy the readers. If you are in a school district with several elementary schools, try to borrow books by the featured authors from the other schools beforehand.

If you plan to have the party in October, tell students they must have their books read before October 26 or 27—you will need a few days to send out the party invitations and make sure the cake will be ready. If the party is to be after October, let the students read until the end of the month. On the day of the party, blow up black and orange balloons for decorations (if possible) and have the cake and small favors ready.

It's always great to have an author come to these parties, but if you cannot secure one, plan a short video or movie or a game like 7-Up. You might want to play appropriate games (such as Authors) or have a contest to see who can find the most words in one of the featured authors' names. If possible, the film or video should be about one of the authors' books. If many read the required number of books, you may need to have two parties—one for primary students and one for older students.

OTHER IDEAS: _____

_____

_____

_____

_____

October Authors

October 3, 1918	Molly Cone
October 3, 1906	Natalie Savage Carlson
October 3, 1948	Marilyn Singer
October 4, 1916	Julia Cunningham
October 4, 1892	Robert Lawson
October 4, 1924	Donald J. Sobol
October 5, 1928	Louise Fitzhugh
October 6, 1941	Steven Kellog
October 7, 1893	Alice Dalgleish
October 8, 1920	Barthe DeClements
October 8, 1937	Johanna Hurwitz
October 10, 1907	Dorothy Shuttlesworth
October 10, 1922	Ann Holm
October 10, 1942	James Marshall
October 14, 1926	Miriam Cohen
October 14, 1928	Polly Cameron
October 20, 1908	Wylly Folk St. John
October 21, 1929	Ursula LeGuin
October 23, 1897	Marjorie Flack
October 24, 1899	Phyllis Fenner
October 24, 1907	Bruno Munari
October 24, 1927	Barbara Robinson
October 27, 1924	Constance C. Greene
October 28, 1921	Leonard Kessler
October 31, 1932	Katherine Paterson
October 31, 1904	Sidney Taylor

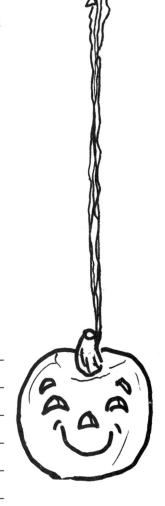

————— OCTOBER CONTEST CORNER —————

The contest corner is often the first place children look when they come to the library, so try to stimulate their minds as well as encourage their use of the library. One contest could be "Who can find the most book titles in our library that contain the word *Halloween?*" If you prefer to deemphasize Halloween, you can substitute the colors red or yellow for the word *Halloween.*

You can also use the mind benders or mind stretchers found in various teacher magazines. The only drawback is that these games are sometimes used in the classroom.

This is a good month for a riddle spot since there are so many riddles for Halloween. Feature several riddles on colorful paper with an appropriate picture. Provide paper so students can write the answers to as many riddles as they can. Be sure to number the riddles, and be sure children number their answers. This contest stimulates a run on the riddle books!

A "Which Witch Would You Choose?" contest may get some students reading fairy tales to find out which witch is which. Make a witch out of colored paper. The envelope containing the contest sheets could be a pocket in her apron. Both the contest sheet and a pattern for the witch are included (the pattern is at the end of this chapter).

Answers to the "Which Witch" contest are as follows:

1. The witch in "Hansel & Gretel"
2. The witch in "Sleeping Beauty"
3. The witch in *The Lion, the Witch and the Wardrobe*
4. The witch in *The Wizard of Oz*
5. The witch in *Strega Nona*
6. The witch in "Snow White and the Seven Dwarfs"

OTHER IDEAS: _____

_____

_____

_____

_____

————— OCTOBER ARTS —————
AND CRAFTS CORNER

Pablo Picasso was born on October 25, so he makes an appropriate artist to feature this month. Put his name (and picture, if you have it) on the bulletin board

WHICH WITCH WOULD YOU CHOOSE?

Witches in fairy tales are sometimes known for doing something really well. If you needed the following things, which witch would you choose to help you?

1. If you are very hungry for a piece of candy or a cookie, which witch might help you?

   _____

2. If you don't like to get up in the morning, which witch might help you?

   _____

3. If winter is your favorite time of year and Turkish Delight is your favorite candy, which witch might help you?

   _____

4. If a high-flying ride on the backs of some winged monkeys sounds like fun to you, which witch should you get in touch with?

   _____

5. If you love macaroni and spaghetti and would like to have all you wanted of them to eat, which witch might help you?

   _____

6. If you are very pretty, which witch should you stay away from?

   _____

The witch in *Strega Nona*   The witch in *The Lion, The Witch and the Wardrobe*   The witch in *The Wizard of Oz*   The witch in *Hansel and Gretel*
The witch in *Snow White and the Seven Dwarfs*   The witch in *Sleeping Beauty*

along with two or three prints of his paintings. You might type a short biography of Picasso to accompany the prints. On the other half of the bulletin board, feature a student artist. Post a photograph of the student (having a Polaroid camera around makes this easy) and write a short paragraph about him or her. If this student is good at crafts or sculpture, place a small table or display case near the bulletin board to display his or her work.

Once the first school artist is featured, many students will want to display their work. Ask each to bring five or six examples of their work for you to see, or consult with the child's teacher as to whether the work is good and original. Be sure it is not copied from a drawing book, something some children love to do. Because of the difference in students' ages and development, you may wish to feature two school artists—one from the primary grades and one from the higher grades.

You might have one or two talented students available in the art corner at noon recess or before and after school to demonstrate or teach a craft to interested students. Masks are an excellent craft to feature this month. Since there probably will not be time to let each student make a mask, ask the demonstrator to show the mask in various stages while explaining how to make it. For example, if it's made on a balloon, show the balloon, then a balloon partially covered with papier mâché, then the full mask without paint, and finally the finished product. Directions could be typed and posted next to an example of each stage.

A form for the school artist's picture and biography is included.

OTHER IDEAS: _____

_____

_____

_____

_____

_____

_____

OCTOBER NONFICTION CORNER

This month the nonfiction corner could feature biographies, especially if you are using the "Whooo Do You Know?" bulletin board. Craft books could also be featured, especially those with Halloween crafts in them such as costume and mask making.

If you have a bulletin board available in this corner, you could feature research questions and offer a prize to any student who independently finds the answers to the research questions and hands them in to you. The caption could simply be

STUDENT ARTIST OF THE MONTH

_____

_____

_____

_____

_____

_____

_____

_____

_____

_____

"October Research." Center each research question on a colorful piece of construction paper or railroad board and put a good-sized jack-o-lantern, bat, black cat, or other appropriate October symbol beside each research question. Since this is early in the year, feature easy research questions that can be answered using either the dictionary or encyclopedia.

Sample questions might be as follows:

- Eleanor Roosevelt was born in October. On what date was she born, and what is one reason she is famous?
- Theodore Roosevelt was a vice-president who became president when the president died. Who was that president?
- The United States got a great bargain when it purchased Alaska on October 18, 1867. From whom was it bought, and how much did it cost?
- Noah Webster was born in October. He is famous for his dictionary. Look up *famous* in a dictionary and give the guide words for the page on which you find it.
- Write the names of two different types of dictionaries found in your school library.

Five questions are usually enough, since the work is to be done independently. Unless many children enter this contest, give a prize that will excite the other children. This will encourage more to do the research questions next month. Take a picture of the research question winners and post it on November's nonfiction bulletin board.

Answers

1. October 11, 1884; answers will vary but may include that she was the wife of Franklin Roosevelt, was a representative to the United Nations, etc.   2. William McKinley, who was assassinated   3. Alaska was purchased from Russia for $7,200,000, about 2¢ an acre.   4. varies depending on dictionary used   5. varies according to school collection

OTHER IDEAS: _____

_____

_____

_____

_____

_____

_____

_____ *OCTOBER SKILLS CLASSES* _____

Students should be very familiar with the library by this time of year, and skills instruction has probably begun in earnest. If you are teaching book location and shelving to any grade, October is an excellent time to have children locate books by pulling all the Halloween books for you to feature during the month. This gives them practice and also saves you time. Call number slips for you to copy and fill in with the Halloween titles in your collection are provided. If you wish, use a colorful sticker in place of the drawings. In either case, if you mount the call slips on tagboard and laminate them, they will last many years. You can add to them or delete from them as necessary. It helps to keep the fiction and nonfiction call slips separate, so you can use the nonfiction call slips with the older students and fiction and easy call slips with younger children.

Provide practice in the use of the card catalog by preparing cards with titles appropriate to the season and asking students to use the card catalog to find the information called for. Two pages of sample cards are provided here. Again, you might want to mount these on tagboard and laminate them so they will last, but if you do this you will need to provide projector pens or china pencils for students to write their answers. Try to use cards calling for books in different drawers of the card catalog so two students will not need the same drawer.

Try to plan each month so one day is saved for book talks or stories and one day for a skills game. The other two sessions can be for regular skills activities. Varying the schedule ensures that students will be eager for their library time.

OTHER IDEAS: _____

_____

_____

_____

_____ *OCTOBER STORYTIMES* _____

If possible, do not begin Halloween stories until the last two weeks in October. There are many good stories that are not about Halloween yet fit in with the "I love to be scared" feeling this month. Some of these titles are listed here.

Harry and the Terrible Whatzit, by Dick Gackenbach. Kindergarten and first-grade students love this story.

Wiley and the Hairy Man, by Molly Bang. Third graders enjoy this story, as will older students if they have not been exposed to it earlier.

Liza Lou and the Yeller Belly Swamp, by Mercer Mayer. All ages enjoy this colorful, exciting book, but it is perhaps most appropriate for second grade.

Bony Legs, by Joanna Cole. Based on a fairy tale, this is a favorite of first and second graders.

BLANK CALL NUMBER SLIPS

Write in call numbers and titles. Use tagboard and laminate.

CARD CATALOG PRACTICE CARDS

Many children dress as ghosts on Halloween Night. Go to the card catalog and look up subject cards for *ghosts*. Write one of the titles:

Write the name of the author:

Have you ever seen a pumpkin fly? One does in *The Mystery of the Flying Orange Pumpkin.* Look up this book in the card catalog and write the name of its author and its publisher:

Bats fly on many nights, not just on Halloween. Go to the card catalog and see if there is a subject card for *bats*. Write the title and author for one book about bats:

Ruth Chew writes many books about witches. Go to the card catalog and write the title and publisher of one of her books:

Black cats may scare you at Halloween, but one gorilla loved a little kitten. Go to the card catalog and write the call number and the authors' name of the book *Koko's Kitten:*

Do spiders scare you? They scare some people! Go to the card catalog and find a subject card for *spiders*. Write the title and copyright date for one of the books about spiders:

CARD CATALOG PRACTICE CARDS continued

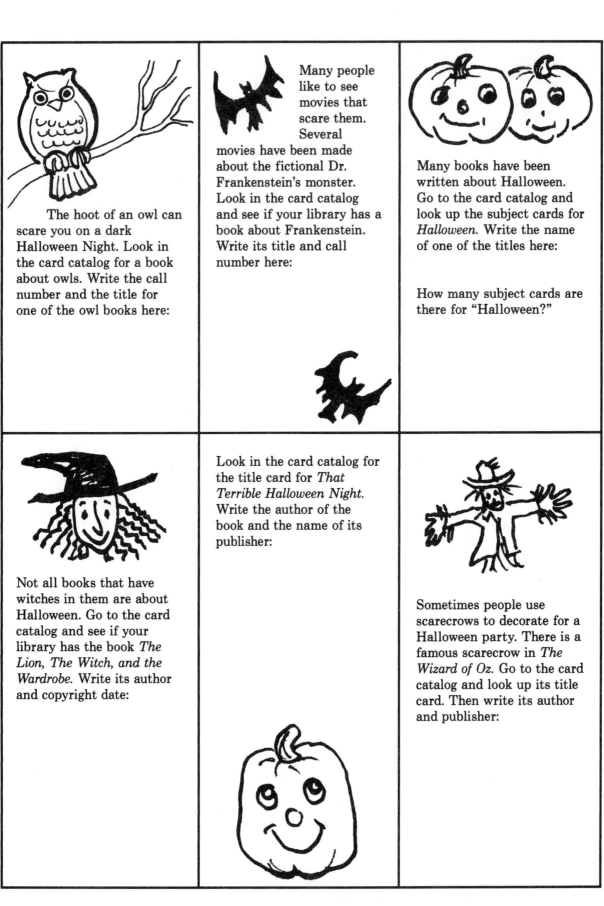

The hoot of an owl can scare you on a dark Halloween Night. Look in the card catalog for a book about owls. Write the call number and the title for one of the owl books here:

Many people like to see movies that scare them. Several movies have been made about the fictional Dr. Frankenstein's monster. Look in the card catalog and see if your library has a book about Frankenstein. Write its title and call number here:

Many books have been written about Halloween. Go to the card catalog and look up the subject cards for *Halloween.* Write the name of one of the titles here:

How many subject cards are there for "Halloween?"

Not all books that have witches in them are about Halloween. Go to the card catalog and see if your library has the book *The Lion, The Witch, and the Wardrobe.* Write its author and copyright date:

Look in the card catalog for the title card for *That Terrible Halloween Night.* Write the author of the book and the name of its publisher:

Sometimes people use scarecrows to decorate for a Halloween party. There is a famous scarecrow in *The Wizard of Oz.* Go to the card catalog and look up its title card. Then write its author and publisher:

The Hobyahs, by B. Parks and J. Smith. This is a "big" book that fascinates first graders and that second graders also enjoy.

Where's the Baby?, by Pat Hutchins. This is the story of characters resembling gnomes or witches, but who have very human characteristics. Grandma thinks baby can do no wrong, but big sister knows better as the family follows baby's hands and footprints through the house. Kindergarten or first-grade students enjoy this story.

Halloween Favorites

Haunted House, by Jan Pienkowski. This is a pop-up book that all ages enjoy. Since it is short, use it as an opener for another story. It is not for check-out, since its complicated pop-ups would not last long.

The Goblins'll Get You, by John Greenleaf Whittier. This is an old favorite. It still sends shivers down the backs of little ones who hear it. It's probably best for grades two and three.

Arthur's Halloween, by Marc Brown. This favorite is also available as a sound filmstrip from Miller Brody. It is well done, and kindergarteners through third-grade students will enjoy the filmstrip as much as the book.

OTHER TITLES YOU LIKE: _____

_____

_____

_____

_____

_____

_____

_____

_____

OCTOBER BOOK TALKS

Because of Halloween, it's always good to feature mystery books in October. Some of the many possibilities are listed here. Be sure to read each book before giving your book talk. You'll find that you enjoy them!

The Dollhouse Murders, by Betty Ren Wright. This book is popular with both boys and girls. It is a suspense mystery with a ghostly conclusion.

The Red Room Riddle, by Scott Corbett. This is also an exciting suspense book. It's about two boys who on Halloween set out to discover whether a nearby house is really haunted.

(Both Corbett and Wright have many other published books, which is a good thing because you can suggest other books by them when students snap up the book you just told them about.)

Encyclopedia Brown, Boy Detective, by Donald J. Sobol. (Or choose any of the other Encyclopedia Brown books.) It's good to introduce this book to third- or fourth-grade students, especially since Sobol's birthday is in October and you can feature him in the authors corner. There are many short mysteries in each book, with the solution to each in the back. Rather than just telling the class about them, read one of the short mysteries and let the class try to solve it.

Rather than a book talk, you might show Pied Piper's sound filmstrip set, "Mysteries," which effectively introduces *The House of Dies Drear,* by Virginia Hamilton, and *The Egypt Game,* by Zilpha Snyder.

There are also broadcasts from public television that feature books, so you can choose one featuring a mystery book and show that. Be sure to have several books by the same author or books of a similar type for students to check out after your book talk, video, or filmstrip. They will want to check out the featured book but can sometimes be satisfied with another related title.

Other mystery and suspense titles that could be the subject of a book talk or other presentation include the following:

Jane-Emily, by Patricia Clapp

Who Stole Kathy Young, by Margaret Goff Clark

Footsteps on the Stairs, by C. S. Adler

The Haunted House, by Peggy Parrish (grades two, three, and perhaps four)

Who Stole Hyacinth McCaw, by Patricia Reilly Giff

OTHER TITLES YOU LIKE: _____

_____

_____

_____

_____

_____

_____

_____

_____

_____

_____

SOME LIBRARY MANAGEMENT FORMS

Hi, _____!
(Class: _____)
The book: _____
_____,
which you asked us to save
for you, is here.

We will save it for you
until _____.

Please let us know if you
no longer wish to have
this book.

FROM THE
LIBRARY

Hi, _____!
(Class: _____)

The following books that you
checked out have not been
returned:

_____

_____

Please return them as soon as possible.
Thank you.

CAN
WE
HELP?

Please let us
know if we
can find
materials
that will
help you.

- - - - - - - - - - - - - - - - - - -

I need materials on:

_____

_____

_____
(teacher)

(Please return to librarian)

A MEMO ON YOUR CLASS'S
PROGRESS IN LIBRARY SKILLS

LMC MANAGEMENT

Overdue Books

By this time, many books have been checked out, and for some the time has come and gone for their return. Don't delay getting a plan in place for the return of overdue books. Sending a frequent, gentle reminder to forgetful students will help prevent a permanent loss of the books.

For libraries with computerized systems, it is a quick and painless procedure to print out overdue lists. These could be done weekly or every other week to be sure students and teachers are aware of books that need to be returned. For libraries without a computer system, getting the message out about overdue books is a time-consuming task, especially in large schools.

If you are using student volunteers as aides in the library, they are not only capable of writing overdue notes to their fellow classmates, they love to do it! Each day, let them write the overdue book reminder notes for books and media that were due on the previous day. A sample page of overdue notes and other library messages is included here. Besides writing these notes, student aides can also cut them apart, sort them into classrooms, and deliver the notes to the appropriate classrooms.

Teachers are your best allies in the constant struggle to see that books are returned on time. For this reason, it is important that they, too, know which students need to return books. Without a computer system, the job is too time-consuming to do weekly or even every other week. However, a once-a-month list of overdue books should be sent to each teacher if at all possible. The daily reminders your students aides have sent will help cut down on the length of the list. These volunteers can also be trained to visit each classroom on the day before you type the list and announce to each class that overdue lists will be typed on the following day. They should ask students to return the books on that day or the following morning. Students often will want to dig out books from their desks and return them immediately, so it is wise for each student aide to carry a box or basket.

Giving a colorful banner to the room with the fewest overdue books can induce students to return books on time. Or you can give a colorful bookmark to each student in the winning room. Rewards like these help to a small degree, but probably the best defense against an increasing list of overdue books is the written reminder notes given to students on a timely basis.

Audiovisual Training

If possible, try to schedule small groups of children into the library so you can instruct them in how to use and take care of the audiovisual equipment. If first-grade teachers in your school send students to the library with free-time passes, then first graders (and any other students new to the equipment) need to be taught how to use and care for the audiovisual materials. Schedule groups of four to six, showing them the proper procedures for using the equipment and the necessity of returning the software to its proper place. If possible, let them practice using the equipment under your supervision. All of this will certainly take time but will be well worth the savings in loss and repairs.

Some LMCs issue a license to operate the various pieces of equipment, with each piece of equipment listed or checked off as the student learns how to use it. This is a good idea, but it is easier to do in a school of two or three hundred than in larger schools. Here is a sample audiovisual license. Adapt it to your own needs and equipment.

AUDIOVISUAL
EQUIPMENT LICENSE

_____

is licensed to use the following equipment:

☐ filmstrip viewers ☐ cassette players

☐ VCR ☐ Dukane filmstrip viewer

_____

Librarian

November

November hints of ice and snow:
Trees are bare and cold winds blow.
Windows are white with frosty lace,
And people walk with quickened pace.

November Calendar

February may be the shortest month according to the calendar, but to many teachers and librarians November seems the shortest. Each week seems to bring some interruption— Veteran's Day, parent-teacher conferences, and Thanksgiving. Conferences often come during National Children's Book Week, interrupting our plans to observe it. With so many interesting things to do in November, the month seems almost too short!

November 1	National Authors Day
November 2, 1889	South Dakota Admission Day
November 2, 1889	North Dakota Admission Day
November 2, 1734	Birthdate of Daniel Boone
November 4, 1922	Tomb of Tutankhamen discovered
November 6, 1861	Birthdate of James Naismith
November 7, 1867	Birthdate of Marie Curie
November 8, 1889	Montana Admission Day
November 9, 1731	Birthdate of Benhamin Banneker
November 11	Veteran's Day
November 11	Canadian Remembrance Day
November 15, 1887	Birthdate of Georgia O'Keeffe
November 15, 1840	Birthdate of Claude Monet
November 16, 1907	Oklahoma Admission Day
November 18, 1901	Birthdate of George Gallup
November 18, 1923	Birthdate of Alan Shepard
November 18, 1928	"Birthdate" of Mickey Mouse
November 19, 1752	Birthdate of George Rogers Clark
November 24, 1864	Birthdate of Toulouse-Lautrec

Check your calendar for exact dates of

American Education Week
National Children's Book Week
Thanksgiving

_____ *NOVEMBER THEMES* _____

Our American Heritage makes a good theme for the month because of the emphasis on our history during the Thanksgiving season. Research questions and bulletin boards can be used to enhance this theme. If you have a secure place to exhibit valuable items, you might want to display antiques that relate to our heritage. You may also be able to find someone who can talk about and demonstrate old-fashioned skills such as spinning, weaving, churning butter, and so on. These talks inspire students to read more books from the history section of the library.

Thanksgiving is a possible theme for bulletin boards. You can use that theme to promote books about the first Thanksgiving and biographies of famous Americans of that time.

I Love Books is a particularly appropriate theme this month because of National Children's Book Week.

OTHER IDEAS: _____

_____

_____

_____

_____ *SPECIAL DAYS IN* _____
NOVEMBER

Children are as fascinated with the pyramids and ancient Egypt as adults are. Since the most famous Egyptian archaeological find, the tomb of Tutankhamen, was made on November 4, 1922, it might be fun to have an Ancient Egypt Week. Ask students to build pyramids from sugar cubes, wooden blocks, etc. and bring them to exhibit in the library. You could show a film like David Macauley's *Pyramid* or a film about ancient Egypt (to classes old enough to understand it). Display a sentence in Egyptian hieroglyphics and challenge students to guess its meaning. Or ask them to develop their own hieroglyphics for an alphabet. Feature both fiction and nonfiction books about Egypt in displays and book talks.

National Children's Book Week offers all kinds of possibilities. How about a book parade? Have students (possibly members of the authors birthday club) make "sandwich" boards advertising a favorite book. The front board (made from railroad or tagboard) should look like the book jacket, with the title, author, and an illustration. The back board should feature a blurb advertising the book. Join the two boards at the top with ribbon or cord on either side, so a student can wear it by putting it over his or her head. Then students parade from room to room advertising books suitable for the class's grade level. One person not

wearing a sandwich board can accompany the group and serve as an announcer, reading the titles of each book as the student wearing the sandwich board steps forward. The announcer can also read the blurb on the back, unless students can do it from memory. When all students have been introduced, they can parade slowly around the room, showing off their advertisements.

This month is a good time to take a poll in each room to find out the students' favorite book. This fits in with both Book Week activities and the birthday of the great pollster, George Gallup, on November 18. First, secure the support of the teachers, and then ask each to poll his or her students about their favorite book. Ask each teacher to have students decorate the classroom door as if it were the book jacket of their favorite book. The students enjoy doing this, and it makes an art activity for the teacher (be sure to give the teacher plenty of lead time, however). Even young students can do this. Kindergarten students can promote books such as *One Fish, Two Fish, Red Fish, Blue Fish,* by Dr. Seuss, or *Fat Cat,* by Jack Kent, very effectively. The teacher might need to make the letters, but the students can do the rest.

When all doors are completed, take pictures of each. If teachers in your school like contests, award ribbons for "Most Creative," "Most Colorful," "Best Use of Materials Other Than Paper," and so on. You can think of a category for almost any door. Teachers might like to take their classes around the school to see the doors, or you can take your classes around as part of your literature appreciation plans.

Disney Day or Mickey Mouse Day can be a fun way to celebrate the first appearance of Mickey Mouse. Students can dress as favorite Disney characters or bring favorite Disney toys. You can also feature many Disney books and videos.

For National Education Week, show the students and parents in your school that teachers and staff have interesting hobbies. Invite the teachers to bring samples of their hobbies to the library for display during this week. You will be surprised at the talents of teachers and staff. Make sure that collections, crafts, artwork, and so on are protected from damage and theft, and discuss with your classes (and the teacher who brought the material) what can and cannot be handled. Next to each, post a sign with the picture of the contributor and a little information about him or her. This makes the display even more interesting to students, parents, and staff.

Other National Education Week ideas: Display textbooks from past years, contrasting them with current texts, or arrange a display of staff pictures from past years.

Choose only one or two of the preceding activities, or you will be overwhelmed since all involve quite a bit of work.

OTHER IDEAS: _____

_____

_____

_____

_____

NOVEMBER BULLETIN BOARDS

"Gobble Up These Great Books" and "Pick a Winner" are the two bulletin boards featured, but November offers many opportunities for other bulletin boards as well. Some possible captions include "Feast on These" (featuring new books),

"Read—It's Fun!" (good for Children's Book Week), "Reading Is a Hobby That Lasts a Lifetime" (also good for Book Week), "Leaf Through These" (make large colored leaves and staple beside each book jacket), "Read About Early America" (history and historical fiction book jackets), and "Read About the First Thanksgiving."

For the "Gobble Up These Great Books" bulletin board, enlarge the turkey included with the patterns at the end of this chapter. (This turkey is also used for the authors birthday club bulletin board, but with less enlargement.) Use light tan construction paper or railroad board if it is available. You can make the turkey more attractive if you color the bill, wattles, legs, and feet. The white of the eye can be filled in with white, and the rest of the turkey can be outlined in black or brown felt-tip pen. Feature book jackets that have food in the title or are about Thanksgiving in some way. If you prefer, use the caption "Gobble Up These Old Favorites" or "Gobble Up These New Books," adjusting the book jackets appropriately.

The book jackets featured in the "Pick a Winner" bulletin board can be sports titles or any favorites in demand from your students.

NOVEMBER AUTHORS
BIRTHDAY CLUB

There are many authors to choose from in November. If you have a large school, it might be best to feature as many of the authors as you can so there will be

November Authors

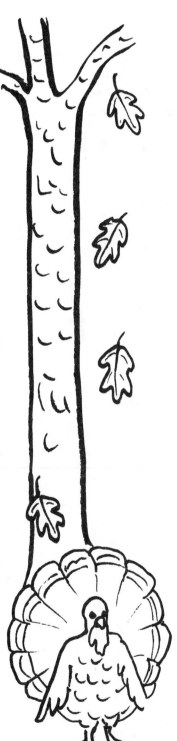

November 2, 1919	Mildred Ames
November 4, 1906	Sterling North
November 8, 1932	Ben Bova
November 8, 1945	Mariana Mayer
November 9, 1937	Lynn Hall
November 12, 1928	Marjorie Weinman Sharmat
November 13, 1850	Robert Louis Stevenson
November 13, 1915	Nathaniel Benchley
November 14, 1907	Astrid Lindgren
November 14, 1907	William Steig
November 15, 1941	Daniel Manus Pinkwater
November 16, 1915	Jean Fritz
November 16, 1952	Robin McKinley
November 16, 1920	Colin Thiele
November 20, 1938	Marion Dane Bauer
November 20, 1919	William Cole
November 21, 1907	Christie Harris
November 21, 1908	Elizabeth George Speare
November 21, 1908	Leo Politi
November 23, 1926	Harold Berson
November 24, 1849	Frances Hodgson Burnett
November 24, 1806	Carlos Collodi
November 24, 1933	Sylvia Engdahl
November 24, 1921	Yoshiko Uchida
November 25, 1946	Marc Brown
November 25, 1909	P. D. Eastman
November 25, 1922	Charles Schulz
November 26, 1901	Doris Gates
November 29, 1832	Louisa May Alcott
November 29, 1898	C. S. Lewis
November 29, 1919	Madeleine L'Engle
November 30, 1835	Mark Twain
November 30, 1667	Jonathan Swift
November 30, 1931	Margot Zemach
November 30, 1874	Lucy Maud Montgomery

books for all who wish to participate. Smaller schools can get away with featuring fewer, especially if they are in a city where schools can borrow from each other.

For the bulletin board, copy the turkey (included in the patterns at the end of this chapter) on tan paper. Color the wattles, beak, and feet with felt-tip pens and add white to the eyes and accents of white to the feathers to make the turkeys even more colorful and appealing. Then put each featured author's name on the breast of the turkey. Place the turkeys around the large cut-out birthday cake. If you used the authors birthday club in October, the cake will already be on the bulletin board. Cut out "November" letters to replace the "October" letters for the caption "Happy Birthday November Authors."

With such favorites as Marc Brown, William Steig, and C. S. Lewis represented, you will probably have quite a few students qualifying for an invitation to the authors birthday party at the end of the month. Plan something that students will really enjoy so others will be enthusiastic about reading in December. A video is popular, but if you can afford it or have a talented volunteer, a storyteller would be both appropriate and popular.

For easy refreshments that do not require plates and forks, offer decorated cupcakes and punch. A reading button or a helium-filled balloon make good gifts for each participant. Since most schools cannot afford large gifts for each student, a drawing for a special prize could be held sometime during the party. Have students write their names on slips of paper as they come for the party. At the end of the party, have someone draw a name for the prize book. Be sure to take pictures of the party for your next authors' birthday bulletin board.

Plan now for December by writing letters to some of the December authors requesting a brief letter to the students.

OTHER IDEAS: _____

_____

_____

_____

_____

———————— NOVEMBER CONTEST ————————
CORNER

To involve the children in scanning either the card catalog or the shelves, offer a prize to the student who can make the longest list of books with some type of food in the title. This relates to the Thanksgiving feast, and students enjoy seeing who can make the longest list. You might wish to award a prize for the student in each grade who has made the longest list, since older students will probably be able to make longer lists than primary students.

Don't forget to post notices of national contests in the contest corner. There are always contests open to students from publishing companies, newspapers, and so on. You probably get many notices of such contests in your mail. Although you may not have many students who enter, it will bring these contests to the notice of some who might wish to try.

Look in November magazines for riddles for your "Riddle Spot" contest. Some months you may wish to use a "Use Your Head" contest instead. Feature thinking-type questions found in magazines for gifted students or in publications that emphasize thinking skills.

OTHER IDEAS: _____

_____

_____

_____

_____

_____

NOVEMBER ARTS AND CRAFTS CORNER

Artists whose work can be featured in November include Claude Monet, born on November 15, 1840; Georgia O'Keeffe, born November 15, 1887; and Henri de Toulouse-Lautrec, born November 24, 1864. Try to find examples of the work of the artist you feature and also mount a picture of him or her and some information about the artist's life. Or ask a student to give a report to various classes about the artist or to make up appropriate research questions.

Books you can feature in this corner this month could be about Early American crafts such as weaving, making corn husk dolls, quilting, knitting, and so on. A demonstration of some of these crafts is fun if you can find someone to do it. There are often people in the community who are willing to come to the schools and demonstrate spinning, weaving, and other Early American crafts.

November is a great time to feature Native American crafts. Having students make God's Eyes is fun and comparatively easy. Prepare crossed sticks (or popsicle sticks) in advance so there will be plenty for any child who wants to learn to weave the God's Eye. The directions for making one can be found in almost any book on weaving. Learn to do it and then teach students; ask the most proficient volunteer to be in the arts and crafts corner at noon recess to teach others the craft. A week before you plan to do this, send notes home asking parents to send in yarn or yarn scraps. Let students take their God's Eyes home or display them in the library.

Don't forget to feature another student artist. Emphasize that they must bring in two or three examples of their best work for you to display. Many children will come in with a quick, hurried drawing, and you must tell them they need several examples; otherwise, you will be bombarded with drawings from everyone.

OTHER IDEAS: _____

_____

_____

_____

_____

NOVEMBER NONFICTION CORNER

The obvious books to feature this month are books on the first Thanksgiving, the Pilgrims, Native Americans, and other early settlers. You might also feature books on immigrants who arrived in our country in later years, such as the Irish, Germans, Mexicans, or Vietnamese, to name just a few. (You can tailor this to your local community.) A bulletin board featuring these books could be captioned "Why America is the Melting Pot of the World."

Research questions for November include the following:

1. Who proclaimed the first national Thanksgiving Day in the United States?
2. Canada also has a Thanksgiving Day. When is it?
3. Oklahoma was admitted to the Union in November. On what date did it become a state?
4. National Book Week is in November. Who wrote the following quotation about books? "And entertains the harmless day with a well-chosen book or friend."
5. Mark Twain, author of *The Adventures of Tom Sawyer,* was born on November 30. In what year was he born, and where was his birthplace?

Answers

1. George Washington in 1789   2. The second Monday in October
3. November 16, 1907   4. Sir Henry Wotton   5. In 1835, in Florida, Missouri

OTHER IDEAS: _____

_____

_____

_____

_____

_____ *NOVEMBER SKILLS CLASSES* _____

Let second, third, or fourth graders pull the Thanksgiving books for you after you put the call numbers and titles on the turkey call slips included here. Make as many slips as you have books (and a few extra for new acquisitions), and after you have filled in call numbers and titles, cut them out and laminate them so they will last. You may want younger students to pull fiction and easy books and older students to pull the numbered nonfiction books.

When choosing activity worksheets to teach skills, look for worksheets that are interesting and not too long. For example, a skills activity using a book of quotations would be interesting and fun for most students if there were four to ten quotations for them to look up (depending on ability). It would be much less fun and no more educational if they had to look up twenty questions instead. If you find an interesting activity but feel it is too long for your students, shorten it before you copy the page.

Are you trying to teach students something about the Dewey Decimal system? Laminate the book covers of many nonfiction books (it helps to mount them first on railroad board). Divide the class into teams and give each team a copy of the Dewey Decimal numbers and what category each number represents (a sheet is provided). Stack all the book jackets and choose the one on top to show to the first team. They have forty seconds (or some other amount that you set) to consult together using the Dewey Decimal sheet and decide what category the book would be in. If their answer is right (the first answer given is all that is allowed), then the team is given the book jacket and you show the next jacket to the next team. If the first team's answer is wrong, the next team has an opportunity to supply the correct Dewey Decimal category. If they also miss, proceed to the next team. If all the teams miss, tell the class the proper category and place the jacket at the bottom of the pile. When the title comes up again, the teams should know it. Proceed through the pile of book jackets until time is up. Each team counts the book jackets it has been awarded, and the team with most is declared the winner. This game, although it does not teach all categories of the Dewey system, does help familiarize students with the different categories and the types of books in them.

OTHER IDEAS: _____

_____

_____

_____

_____

_____

_____

THANKSGIVING CALL NUMBER SLIPS

THE DEWEY DECIMAL SYSTEM

000–099	**GENERAL REFERENCE:** Encyclopedias, bibliographies, "maybe" subjects like U.F.O.'s, the Loch Ness Monster, Bigfoot, etc.
100–199	**PHILOSOPHY:** Ethics, the occult, astrology, ghosts, psychology, philosophy
200–299	**RELIGION:** Different religions, churches, the Bible, myths
300–399	**SOCIAL STUDIES:** Government, law, warfare, education, transportation, customs, holidays, fairy tales, folk tales, legends, costume
400–499	**LANGUAGES:** Dictionaries, sign languages, various languages, grammars, alphabets
500–599	**PURE SCIENCE:** Mathematics, physics, geology, meteorology, weather, fossils, ecology, botany, zoology
600–699	**TECHNOLOGY (Applied Science):** Inventions, medicine, health, diseases, engineering, crops, foods, cooking, domestic animals, pets, manufacturing
700–799	**FINE ARTS AND LEISURE TIME:** Architecture, dwellings, drawing, art appreciation, crafts, games, hobbies, sports, music, dance
800–899	**LITERATURE:** Drama, poetry, humor (jokes and riddles), collections of stories
900–999	**HISTORY:** Geography, travel, biography, history

NOVEMBER STORYTIMES

William Steig is one of the birthday authors for this month, so it might be appropriate to read some of his books during storytime. His books seem best for second or third grade, although the vocabulary is often above even these students. They understand the stories, however, and really enjoy them.

Sylvester and the Magic Pebble, by William Steig, is a Caldecott winner and great fun to read. As a warm-up activity, you could play Twenty Questions with a polished red pebble as the object to guess. If you can afford it, a polished pebble or a piece of rock candy for each student after the story is exciting.

Doctor DeSoto, also by Steig, is especially enjoyed by second graders. Expect them to try to say "Frank yu very mush," as the fox does when his teeth are glued together by the wily Dr. DeSoto.

Brave Irene, by Steig, is a good one to read to third graders and is appropriate this month as snow begins to fall in many parts of the country.

Arthur's Thanksgiving, by Marc Brown, is obviously appropriate because of the holiday and even more so because the author's birthday is this month. Any of his Arthur books will be appreciated by students in the primary grades.

A simple crafts book would be good to show to second or third graders. Letting them try one of the crafts in the book would be fun if you have the room to do so. Be sure to have other crafts books available, for many students will want to check out one.

OTHER TITLES YOU LIKE: _____

_____

_____

_____

_____

_____

_____

_____

_____

NOVEMBER BOOK TALKS

November, with its emphasis on our early heritage, is a good time to feature historical fiction books.

The Sign of the Beaver, by Elizabeth Speare. This book is about a young boy of early America who is left behind in a newly built cabin when his father goes to their old home to bring back the rest of his family. The boy is duped out of his gun by a frightening stranger and then has a devastating encounter with bees. Some friendly Indians help him, and he teaches them English. Students in grade five and above enjoy this book.

Caddie Woodlawn, by Carol Ryrie Brink. This is an old favorite also available in audiovisual form, including videocassette.

The Matchlock Gun, by Walter Edmonds. This is another old favorite also available on videocassette and in filmstrip sets.

Roanoke, by Sonia Levitin. It's best to feature this book in older classes—probably grade six and above. It tells the story of the lost colony of Roanoke.

The Upstairs Room, by Joanna Reiss. This is a fictionalized story of the author's actual experiences as a Jewish child during World War II. Books about this era should be especially in demand during the years 1991 to 1995 since these years mark the fiftieth anniversary of the events of World War II. There will undoubtedly be new ones published during these years that you might wish to feature.

OTHER TITLES YOU LIKE: _____

_____

_____

_____

_____

_____

_____

_____

_____

_____ *LMC MANAGEMENT* _____

Audiovisual Check-Out Management

Is your audiovisual check-out system working well? Machines that break down and need repairs cause other problems when teachers who are missing the broken machines borrow from other teachers' classrooms, bypassing your system. If material is stored in classrooms and checked out to that classroom, emphasize to teachers that the borrowed equipment must be returned to the assigned room after *each* use. If this is not done, the assigned teachers will come to you and say that the equipment assigned to them is missing, and you will have to go from classroom to classroom to find it. If you have a room where equipment can be stored, you can avoid this problem. In any case, try to conduct an occasional equipment class so teachers are familiar with all of the school's audiovisual equipment and how to use it properly.

If you have not already done so, be sure to set a policy on individual check-out of equipment. If your school has a camcorder and teachers are allowed to check it out for personal use, how do you decide who gets to check it out during the Christmas vacation or at Halloween or other holidays? Also, when teachers are allowed to take the equipment for their own personal use, the equipment is not always returned on time and some classrooms may not get to use it as planned. It is much simpler and makes a great deal more sense to allow no check-out of equipment for private use. Most teachers will understand that the equipment is expensive and was purchased for school use, not individual pleasure.

Ordering

By now your desk or work counters are probably piled high with catalogs that you do not want to throw away until you have gone through them. If time permits, try to go through one each day and tear out (if you are the only person using the catalog) anything you are interested in for your want file. Look through brochures quickly; if you like the material, order immediately or place in your want file. The brochures that do not interest you should go in the wastebasket. Catalogs from major suppliers should probably be filed alphabetically, in case you hear of some item you wish to order later. As you or your aide file each catalog, be sure to toss old issues.

In most school districts, it is best to order materials fairly early in the year, because money not spent by a certain time is consigned to the general fund, and you will lose it. Therefore, check your want file frequently and order what you need as soon as possible. This way, you can use the material during the year.

December

How many days 'til Christmas?
I wonder if you know?
One day of cookie baking,
One shopping day in snow.
One day of present wrapping,
One day to trim the tree,
One day for a grade school pageant,
How many can that be?
One day to drive around the town,
And see lighted houses on the blocks,
One day for writing Christmas cards,
One day to hang our socks.
Now let me see how much is that?
I'll count them out and see.
Only eight days left 'til Christmas,
And that's too long a wait for me!

December Calendar

Winter holidays make December a short month at school. Autumn is over and winter begins.

December 2, 1859	Birthdate of artist Georges Pierre Seurat
December 3, 1818	Illinois entered the Union
December 3, 1775	Birthdate of artist Gilbert Charles Stuart
December 5, 1782	Birthdate of President Martin Van Buren
December 5, 1830	Birthdate of poet Christina Rossetti
December 5, 1901	Birthdate of Walt Disney
December 6	St. Nicholas Day
December 7, 1941	Pearl Harbor bombed
December 8, 1765	Birthdate of inventor Eli Whitney
December 8, 1886	Birthdate of artist Diego Rivera
December 10, 1830	Birthdate of poet Emily Dickinson
December 10, 1817	Mississippi entered the Union
December 11, 1816	Indiana entered the Union
December 12, 1787	Pennsylvania entered the Union
December 14, 1819	Alabama entered the Union
December 14, 1911	South Pole first reached
December 15	Bill of Rights Day
December 16, 1773	Boston Tea Party
December 17, 1903	Wright brothers' flight at Kitty Hawk, North Carolina
December 18, 1787	New Jersey entered the Union
December 18, 1879	Birthdate of artist Paul Klee
December 20	Louisiana Purchase Day
December 21, 1620	Pilgrims landed at Plymouth, Massachusetts
December 21	First day of winter
December 21, 1913	First crossword puzzle published
December 25	Christmas Day, birthdate of Maurice Utrillo (1883)
December 25, 1821	Birthdate of Clara Barton
December 28, 1846	Iowa entered the Union
December 29, 1856	Birthdate of President Woodrow Wilson
December 29, 1845	Texas entered the Union
December 29, 1808	Birthdate of President Andrew Johnson
December 31	New Year's Eve, birthdate of artist Henri Matisse (1869)

Check your calendar for the exact date of

Hanukkah

DECEMBER THEMES

Since winter break is in December, the month is a short one. Your theme could be *Home for the Holidays* and emphasize the different customs that abound in different homes. For this, feature Hanukkah as well as some of the many Christmas customs. Focus on books about the holidays in our country and in other countries. *December—an Exciting Month in History* could also be a theme, since so many exciting events happened in history this month. Along with this theme, you could emphasize the nine states that entered the Union in December, Pearl Harbor Day, the historic flight of the Wright brothers, the South Pole finally reached, and the birthdays of many famous people.

OTHER IDEAS: _____

_____

_____

_____

_____

_____

SPECIAL DAYS IN DECEMBER

December is such a busy month that you may not wish to have any additional special days. However, there are possibilities for some special days if you want to have them.

A Walt Disney Day would be appropriate for December 5, his birthday. Display all the books you have with Disney characters. Ask children to bring any Disney characters they have for you to display—many have stuffed toys, ceramic curios, and so on. Pictures of students taken at Disney World or Disneyland can be an eye-catching part of the display. You might have a student or students research how many movies Walt Disney made from published books (not books published after the movie). A picture of Disney and his biography could be featured near the displays.

A poetry day would be appropriate in honor of both Christina Rossetti and Emily Dickinson. Encourage teachers to read poetry on this day, and feature books of poetry in the library. Read a favorite poem by either Rossetti or Dickinson in each library class and tell something about the poet. You could also display an old poetry volume from the past, if you have one, and then show children some of the beautiful and entertaining poetry books for children published today.

The Boston Tea Party or the flight of the Wright brothers could generate interesting special days, too.

OTHER IDEAS: _____

_____

_____

_____

_____

_____

_____

DECEMBER BULLETIN BOARDS

"Is a Book on Your List?" would emphasize some of the students' favorite books. Ask a class or perhaps your library aides to give you the titles of their favorite books. Write the name of the student and his or her favorite book on Santa's list. The rest of the board can be decorated with colorful book jackets of favorite books, each tied with a red or green bow before being mounted on the bulletin board.

Another appropriate bulletin board could be "Come In from the Cold and Read!" Cut out lacy snowflakes from white tissue paper. Mount them on a bright or dark blue bulletin board along with the bear and assorted book jackets. Cut the bear from brown construction paper and his hat, scarf, and boots from brightly colored paper. Make the books he is carrying real book jackets. Cut letters or use pin-back plastic letters. This bulletin board is good for any winter month.

DECEMBER AUTHORS BIRTHDAY CLUB

December has many popular authors. Choose as many as you need for the size of your school and the available books. Put each author's name on the card held by the teddy bear (the pattern is at the end of this chapter) and position the bears around the birthday cake. Adding a sprig of holly to the cake will make it more festive. If you have been using autumn colors for your letters or background, you may wish to switch to red or blue—colors that can be used for all the winter months.

At each storytime and library skills class, introduce the authors appropriate to the students' grade level. Show the students some of the authors' books and explain the authors birthday club to them. You may wish to shorten the time allowed for reading and require that the students return the books before winter break; or you may let the students read over the winter break. If the party is before the break, you can use favors or small gifts appropriate to the season. If you choose to have the party in early January, snowman decorations would be appropriate.

December Authors

December 2, 1946	David Macaulay
December 5, 1919	Jim Kjelgaard
December 5, 1933	Harve Zemach
December 8, 1919	Kin Platt
December 9, 1937	Mary Downing Hahn
December 9, 1938	Joan Blos
December 9, 1918	Jerome Beatty, Jr.
December 9, 1915	Elouise Jarvis McGraw
December 10, 1903	Mary Norton
December 14, 1929	Lorna Balian
December 18, 1927	Marilyn Sachs
December 19, 1928	Eve Bunting
December 20, 1936	Carol Farley
December 22, 1917	William O. Steele
December 23, 1937	Avi
December 23, 1932	Richard Kennedy
December 24, 1931	Margaret Anderson
December 24, 1897	Noel Streatfield
December 25, 1915	Eth Clifford
December 26, 1937	Jean Van Leeuwen
December 28, 1895	Carol R. Brink
December 28, 1928	Janet Lunn
December 28, 1919	Emily Neville
December 29, 1943	Molly Garrett Bang
December 29, 1943	Irene Brady
December 30, 1922	Jane Langton
December 30, 1805	Rudyard Kipling
December 30, 1943	Mercer Mayer
December 30, 1933	Alvin Silverstein

After-Christmas sales sometimes provide inexpensive items that can be used for a prize drawing. You may be able to find appropriate pencils or eraser tops for each book club winner.

OTHER IDEAS: _____

_____

_____

_____

_____

DECEMBER CONTEST CORNER

Because the first crossword puzzle appeared in December, you might hold a contest to see who can make the best crossword puzzle. Show the children how to do it, and provide graph paper for them. If you feel that crossword puzzles are too difficult, provide graph paper but ask the students to make a wordsearch, another form of the crossword puzzle. Give prizes to the student at each grade level who can use the most book characters in a wordsearch. If you have time, you can do this during a classtime in the library. Or use the December crossword count* provided here as a contest to see which student can get the most points.

Another contest: Put a book in a box and wrap it up nicely. Post a riddle about the book. The first child to guess the riddle wins the book. You can display a different wrapped book and riddle each week of school in December. For example, "This book has a character in it who is always in a crowd. This book has a call number of Fic, Ha." (Answer: *Where's Waldo?,* by Martin Handley). If no one has guessed the book title by Wednesday, add another clue, such as "The main character in this book wears a stocking cap," or "The main character in this book is very hard to find." Take a picture of the winner and put it on your contest bulletin board.

An activity that asks who can make the longest list of book titles containing either the word *winter* or the word *snow* gets students searching the shelves and card catalog.

OTHER IDEAS: _____

_____

_____

_____

_____

DECEMBER ARTS AND CRAFTS CORNER

Famous artists born in December whose work and biographies can be displayed in the art corner include Georges Seurat, Gilbert Charles Stuart, Diego Rivera, Paul Klee, Maurice Utrillo, and Henri Matisse. Display the works of one or several of these exceptional artists. Or, since some of the most famous art masterpieces of the world depict the Nativity, display some copies of these instead. Try to avoid the appearance of endorsing a particular religion, however, especially if this is an issue in your school.

If you are using *Home for the Holidays* as a theme, display student drawings of how they spend the holidays in their homes. At the end of November, ask students to bring in drawings or paintings of the holiday as they celebrate it. Display the best in the art corner, but also display all that are turned in, either in the hall or on another bulletin board.

You can also display decorations made by the students. Encourage students to find a decoration in one of the library's craft books, make it, and then bring it to you for display in this corner.

---

*Other crossword counts are available from Quailridge Media, Selma, Oregon.

Crossword Fun

See how high a score you can get on this crossword puzzle by using letters with high point values. Each letter listed on the right side of the page has a point value. Find words that use high-point letters to fill the puzzle. Then total your points. No proper nouns may be used. Look in the dictionary to find words that will give you a good score. Have fun!

LETTER POINTS

A:	17
B:	16
C:	15
D:	14
E:	13
F:	12
G:	11
H:	10
I:	9
J:	8
K:	7
L:	18
M:	19
N:	20
O:	25
P:	22
Q:	2
R:	21
S:	23
T:	26
U:	20
V:	4
W:	5
X:	6
Y:	24
Z:	1

T	O	Y	S
1.			2.
3.			4.
5.	6.	7.	8.

YOUR SCORE: BOX 1: _____ BOX 2: _____ BOX 3: _____

BOX 4: _____ BOX 5: _____ BOX 6: _____

BOX 7: _____ BOX 8: _____ TOTAL: _____

OTHER IDEAS: _____

_____

_____

_____

_____

_____ *DECEMBER NONFICTION* _____
CORNER

Display nonfiction holiday books, including books about Hanukkah and celebrations in other lands.

For December research, you can enlarge or reduce the bear pattern at the end of this chapter and write research questions on the card in the bear's paws. Color the bear with felt-tip pens and laminate for future use. You can use one large bear and have a different research question each week, or make several smaller bears and post all the research questions for the entire month. Some research questions for this month include the following:

1. When will Christmas Day be celebrated in the year 2010?
2. Our twenty-eighth president was born on December 28, 1856. What was his name?
3. The bombing of Pearl Harbor sparked the United States' entry into World War II. Where is Pearl Harbor?
4. Illinois, Alabama, and Mississippi are three states that entered the Union in December. Which became a state first?
5. Indiana, Pennsylvania, and Texas also entered the Union in December. Which became a state last?

Answers

1. Saturday (Use the perpetual calendar in the *World Almanac.*)   2. Woodrow Wilson   3. Hawaii   4. Mississippi, on December 10, 1817   5. Texas, on December 29, 1845

OTHER IDEAS: _____

_____

_____

_____

_____

BLANK CALL NUMBER SLIPS

Write in call numbers and titles. Use tagboard and laminate.

DECEMBER SKILLS _CLASSES_

Use the holidays as a springboard for your skills classes. Have third and fourth graders practice finding books by pulling your holiday books for you. You can put the call numbers and titles on the ornament designs provided. Copy them on colored paper and highlight with felt-tip pens, or have the students color them for you. Mount them on tagboard and then laminate, after you have written in the call numbers and titles. This activity gives students practice in locating books, and it will save you time each holiday season.

Fourth, fifth, and sixth graders can use the almanac to learn how to use the perpetual calendar. Have them look up such dates as their birthdays in the next year or in the year 2025, or have them see what day of the week will be Christmas Day in a given year.

Practice using maps in an atlas by dividing students into teams and seeing which team can find out what state they are in if they spend the holidays at a certain location. It is relatively early in the year, so use the grid; for example, ask "What state are you in if you are at D-10?" Later in the year, add latitude and longitude.

Provide dictionary practice for grades two, three, and four by asking students to quickly locate holiday words such as *menorah, candle, holly, gift,* and so on. You can write the words on the board or on a worksheet, but sometimes it is good to have the students work without pencil and paper. Give the word and see how quickly students can find it. Then ask one student to give the guide words on the page, another to read the meaning, and another to tell the part of speech.

Older students can use a book of quotations to find a quotation about the holidays. Let each student or group of students read one quotation.

OTHER IDEAS: _____

_____

_____

_____

_____

_____ _DECEMBER STORYTIMES_ _____

New stories about the holidays appear each year. You will find that one year you discover a good story to use for storytime, and by the next year every classroom teacher is reading that story. For this reason, try to use either new stories you have recently discovered, or go back into your file and use old ones that may have been forgotten. Some of the many delightful stories you could read to your classes include *How the Grinch Stole Christmas,* by Dr. Seuss (one of those titles that are so old they are sometimes forgotten), *Petunia's Christmas,* by Roger Duvoisin, *Arthur's Christmas,* by Marc Brown, and *The Polar Express,* by Chris Van Allsburg. These are all older titles with which you are probably familiar, listed only so that you will not overlook them.

Newer titles appropriate for December include the following:

Hershel and the Hanukkah Goblins, by Eric Kimmel, illustrated by Trina Schart Hyman. A Caldecott Honor Book, this is best for grades two and three.

Be Kind to Your Dog at Christmas, by Barbara Heine Costikyan. This is a book of Christmas superstitions. It is perfect for grade three, although older students will be interested in some of the Christmas folklore and superstitions.

The Year of the Perfect Christmas Tree, by Gloria Houston. This is ideal for grades two and three.

The Christmas Wolf, by Michel Gay. A wolf father finds a way to bring a merry Christmas to his family, but not in the way he had planned. This story is good for kindergarten or first grade.

Max's Christmas and *The Disappearing Bag,* both by Rosemary Wells. These are two short books that delight kindergarten children.

It's Christmas, by Jack Prelutsky. This is a book of holiday poems sure to please first-grade and kindergarten children.

OTHER TITLES YOU LIKE: _____

_____

_____

_____

_____

_____

_____

_____

_____ DECEMBER BOOK TALKS _____

With the short amount of time available in December, you may have to decide whether you want to have book talks this month or suspend them in favor of skills classes. If you do have them, here are a few holiday books you may wish to feature.

The Best Christmas Pageant Ever, by Barbara Robinson. At one time, many teachers read this to students, but it seems to have been forgotten lately. It's much too amusing to forget, so tell the students about it or even read part of it to them.

The House Without a Christmas Tree, by Gail Rock. This is another book once popular and now almost forgotten. It is a story children can relate to of a girl whose father would not allow any holiday joy in his house.

Maggie Forevermore, by Joan Lowery Nixon. This is a story of a girl who is forced to spend Christmas with her father and his new wife.

Some picture books that students in all grades enjoy (and that older students probably understand better than the primary children) are *The Polar Express,* by Chris Van Allsburg and *Hershel and the Hanukkah Goblins,* by Eric Kimmel, illustrated by Trina Schart Hyman.

Don't forget to get out some of your most attractive and interesting nonfiction holiday books to show students. Craft books, cookbooks, and holiday custom books are all interesting to the students. Read a few of the interesting holiday superstitions from *Be Kind to Your Dog at Christmas,* by Barbara Heine Costikyan, and then invite students to write about a holiday custom or superstition and tell how it might have developed.

OTHER TITLES YOU LIKE: _____

_____

_____

_____

_____

_____ *LMC MANAGEMENT* _____

Author's Visit

If you haven't already scheduled a visit by an author and you plan to, don't wait any longer. If you have the money available (from your budget, a book fair, or your PTA), a visit from an author is a very rewarding experience, both for you and the students. However, if you want the author to visit on a specific date, it is essential to schedule early. National Children's Book Week and National Library Week are times in which authors are heavily scheduled. If you want someone for National Library Week in April, schedule it now.

If your funds make it possible, try to schedule one author for the primary grades and another for the older students. Fees for authors vary. Popular authors of many published books charge anywhere from a hundred to several hundred dollars a day. They also expect mileage. When you contact the authors, they will usually tell you how many times they will speak to groups during their visit and also the number of students they prefer to have in the audience. Newly published authors in your vicinity will be much less expensive. Some, with perhaps only one published book, might come and speak just for mileage; a local author might visit free of charge.

Prepare for authors' visits by consulting with them concerning the specific times they will be at your school, what they wish to do for lunch, whether they will have their books for children to purchase, and whether they will have a question-and-answer period at the end of their talk. Also ask them to make clear to you their policies on autographs. Will they autograph only books purchased at this visit, or will they autograph previously purchased books? Authors often prefer not to autograph slips of paper, due to time constraints. Explain the authors' autographing policies to students before the visit.

Prepare the students and staff for the visit by telling them about the author(s) and the visit at least a month before the scheduled time. Encourage teachers to read one of the author's books to appropriate grade levels. Encourage students to read as many of the author's books as possible so they may better enjoy the author's talk and be able to ask intelligent questions. If the author agrees, it is fun to let students who have read at least two of the author's books eat lunch with the author at a special table set up in the library.

A week before the author's visit, send a note home to the parents telling them about the author, his or her books, and the scheduled visit to your school. (Some authors provide you with a sample letter you can adapt to your needs.) If the author plans to have books available for sale and for autographing, be sure to tell them this, including the price of the book. If you have enough space, invite the parents to join their children for the author's visit.

On the day of the visit, be prepared to greet the author and clarify the plans for the day. (You should pay the author at the end of the visit.) Prepare a short introduction, or ask a student to make the introduction.

Many authors are as good at speaking to children as they are at writing for them, so students will probably be excited and happy about the author, his or her books, and the visit. Ask a teacher to have his or her class write a thank-you note to the author, expressing how much they enjoyed the visit, or ask an individual student to do this.

You can also arrange inspiring visits from illustrators of children's books. Illustrators make interesting speakers, and they often bring samples of their work or even draw or paint during their talk. Check to see if you have an illustrator of children's books in your area. If so, follow the same procedures outlined for authors.

Santa's Book List:

December_____

January

January comes with icy feet,
Snowy breath on every street,
Its winter joys can't be denied:
Skiing, skating, a bobsled ride!

January Calendar

January usually begins with a rather let-down feeling for both students and teachers. The holidays are over, and it seems a long time until summer vacation. Try to overcome the January blues with exciting activities in the library—activities that begin as soon as possible after school begins.

January 1	New Year's Day; Rose Bowl and other football games played
January 1, 1735	Birthdate of Paul Revere
January 1, 1752	Birthdate of Betsy Ross
January 2, 1788	Georgia ratified the U.S. Constitution
January 3, 1793	Birthdate of activist Lucretia Mott
January 4, 1809	Birthdate of Louis Braille
January 4, 1869	Utah entered the Union
January 5, 1878	Birthdate of Carl Sandburg
January 6, 1412	Birthdate of Joan of Arc
January 7, 1800	Birthdate of President Millard Fillmore
January 9, 1788	Connecticut ratified the U.S. Constitution
January 9, 1913	Birthdate of President Richard Nixon
January 15, 1892	Basketball rules first published
January 15, 1929	Birthdate of Dr. Martin Luther King, Jr.
January 15, 1967	First Superbowl game played
January 17, 1706	Birthdate of Benjamin Franklin
January 18, 1782	Birthdate of Daniel Webster
January 19, 1807	Birthdate of Robert E. Lee
January 19, 1839	Birthdate of artist Paul Cézanne
January 21, 1813	Birthdate of John C. Fremont
January 21, 1824	Birthdate of Stonewall Jackson
January 23, 1832	Birthdate of artist Edouard Manet
January 26, 1837	Michigan entered the Union
January 27, 1756	Birthdate of Wolfgang Amadeus Mozart
January 28, 1737	Birthdate of Thomas Paine
January 29, 1843	Birthdate of President William McKinley
January 29, 1861	Kansas entered the Union
January 30, 1882	Birthdate of President Franklin D. Roosevelt
January 31, 1919	Birthdate of Jackie Robinson, major league baseball's first black player

© 1991 by The Center for Applied Research in Education

_____ *JANUARY THEMES* _____

Many writers of traditional and modern fairy tales and fantasy were born in January. Jakob Grimm, Charles Perrault, J. R. R. Tolkien, Lewis Carrol, Lloyd Alexander, and other fantasy writers were all born in January, making it a good month to use fantasy themes. These include *Let Your Imagination Fly with Fantasy, Let Books Take You to Fantasyland, From Once Upon a Time to They Lived Happily Ever After,* and *Science Fiction—An Imaginary Look into the Future.*

Fantasyland

Use fantasy stories for both storytimes and book talks, and decorate the library as a fantasyland. Hold a fairy-tale character day, or have a day of fairy-tale foods in the cafeteria. Center contests around fairy tales and fantasy, and publish a fairy-tale newspaper.

Some ideas for decorating the library: Turn your door into an entrance to Fantasyland by making gray paper stones and putting them around the door as if it were a castle wall. Above the door post a computer- or hand-lettered sign proclaiming, "Entrance to Fantasyland." Cut out vines of paper and hang them, or use actual plastic vines and flowers to make the wall more attractive.

If you have any posts or poles in your facility, cover one of them with large construction paper leaves for a Jack-in-the-Beanstalk vine. To further this idea, make giant footprints of black cardboard and place them on the floor leading to the fairy-tale section of the library. Place signs along the way that say, "Follow the giant's footprints to Fairy-tale Land." Above the fairy-tale/folk-tale section, place a large sign that says, "Read These Books and They Will Take You To Fantasyland."

If you like, dress as a fairy-tale character for one or two days during the month—you might dress as a witch, a fairy godmother, a giant, or Jack and the Beanstalk.

Challenge and amuse students by asking them to guess the identity of a mystery fairy-tale character each week, based on clues you give. For example, you could ask the following:

Who is this fairy-tale character? This person is small and has a very bad temper. This person likes to play guessing games. This person likes babies. (Answer: Rumpelstiltskin)

You can give a small prize to every student who guesses the correct character, or give one clue each day until someone correctly identifies the character and give a larger prize to that first student.

Fairy-Tale Newspaper

Students will have fun writing fairy-tale news and reading it. You can either ask one of your skills classes to write the articles or ask a classroom teacher to have her students do it. Give them an example, such as the following, so they will understand how to do it.

HELP NEEDED
Mrs. T. Sole, recently of 211 Fairy-tale Lane, has been forced to make her home in an abandoned shoe after her house was destroyed by fire. She and her many children are very crowded, and there is nothing in the house to eat except bread. She is trying to find shelter.
A fund has been set up for her and her children. If you are interested and would care to contribute, send gold coins to the National Bank of Fairyland.

Explain that the news articles are to be written like actual newspaper articles and that they can be about fairy-tale characters or nursery-rhyme characters. You can use a word processing program to produce the newspaper if you have a computer.

Another idea is to read *The Jolly Postman*, by Janet Ahlberg. Let students write their own letters from fairy-tale characters to other fairy-tale characters. Then make a folder of these fairy-tale letters so others can read them.*

OTHER IDEAS: _____

_____

_____

_____

---

*For other ideas for fairy-tale activities, see "Winter Activities" in *Ready-to-Use Reading Bingos, Puzzles and Research Activities for the Elementary School Year*, published by The Center for Applied Research in Education.

_____ *SPECIAL DAYS IN JANUARY* _____

Martin Luther King, Jr. Day

Make a bulletin board of famous people who are members of minority races in our country. Pictures can be found of many different people, such as Maria Tallchief, Martin Luther King, Jr., Harriet Tubman, Connie Chung, Bill Cosby, Jim Thorpe, etc. You could use this board as a skills activity by asking the students to identify each person using clues posted near each picture. It will be easier for students to use the research tools if you put the name of the person with each picture, asking students to explain why that person is famous.

Another idea for this day is to read students part of King's famous "I Have a Dream" speech, or show a video of it. Then have students write an essay on what their dreams are for this country.

Other Days

For the birthday of Louis Braille, invite someone to demonstrate the use of braille for the blind. Prepare the students by telling them about the life of Louis Braille and encouraging some to read *The Touch of Light,* by Anne E. Neimark, a biography of Braille.

For the Chinese New Year, ask someone knowledgeable about Chinese culture to come in and tell the students about it. He or she could talk about the New Year celebrations or explain the Chinese zodiac, which is comparable to our zodiac. The Chinese zodiac can also make for an interesting bulletin board (one is discussed in the next section). Make sure students realize that both zodiacs represent superstitious beliefs, not science.

OTHER IDEAS: _____

_____

_____

_____

_____

_____ *JANUARY BULLETIN* _____
BOARDS

If you want the bulletin boards to relate to a fairy-tale or fantasy theme, you might want to use the "Make a Wish for a Good Book" design. Enlarge the fairy godmother to a size suitable for your board. Color with felt-tip pens, and use silver or gold glitter on her crown and her wand. The stars that highlight each fairy-tale or fantasy book jacket can also be covered with glitter. The same patterns for the fairy godmother and the stars can be used with the caption "Make a Wish." Give the students colored stars on which to write their wishes. "Make a Wish for the New Year" is another possibility for the caption.

The Chinese zodiac bulletin board is fun for most students, since they like to see which animal year is the year of their birth. If you have books about the Chinese New Year or the zodiac, these jackets could be displayed on either side of the caption.

Other ideas for bulletin boards in January: Use "Make This a Great Year—Read!" along with New Year bells on which you print the year. Post book jackets of either new books or books that fit the month's theme. Or outline a large castle. Each time a student reads a book of fairy tales or fantasy, give him or her a gray stone to glue on the castle. With luck, the castle will be completed by the time the month is over. The caption could be, "Help Complete This Fairy-tale Castle." Less colorful, but easier, would be to outline the stones on the castle and, as students complete a book, have them write their names in the stones and perhaps outline it in black or gray.

OTHER IDEAS: _____

_____

_____

_____

_____

JANUARY AUTHORS
BIRTHDAY CLUB

Introduce the January authors to the appropriate classes and encourage the students to participate. Choose the authors you particularly like so your enthusiasm will be transferred to the students. There are many authors to choose from, so decide how many you need for the size of your school. Be sure to post pictures of last month's authors birthday party on the bulletin board or near it. This encourages other students to participate.

January Authors

January 2, 1932	Jean Little
January 2, 1920	Isaac Asimov
January 2, 1921	Crosby Bonsall
January 3, 1934	Patricia Lee Gauch
January 3, 1892	J.R.R. Tolkien
January 3, 1898	Carolyn Reynolds Naylor
January 4, 1785	Jakob Grimm
January 8, 1921	Lee Ames
January 9, 1944	Clyde Bulla
January 10, 1929	Remy Charlip
January 11, 1931	Mary Rodgers
January 11, 1918	Robert C. O'Brien
January 12, 1628	Charles Perrault
January 12, 1876	Jack London
January 13, 1926	Michael Bond
January 14, 1886	Hugh Lofting
January 17, 1938	John Bellairs
January 18, 1934	Raymond Briggs
January 18, 1882	A. A. Milne
January 19, 1925	Nina Bawden
January 21, 1928	Carol Beach York
January 22, 1930	Brian Wildsmith
January 25, 1914	James Flora
January 26, 1884	Roy Chapman Andrews
January 26, 1831	Mary Mapes Dodge
January 27, 1832	Lewis Carroll
January 27, 1923	Jean Merrill
January 29, 1943	Rosemary Wells
January 29, 1915	Bill Peet
January 29, 1930	Christopher Collier
January 30, 1924	Lloyd Alexander
January 31, 1941	Gerald McDermott

OTHER IDEAS: _____

_____

_____

_____

_____

_____ *JANUARY CONTEST CORNER* _____

In keeping with the fantasy/fairy-tale theme, you can run guessing contests based on mystery fairy-tale or fantasy characters (see the section on themes in this chapter). Or duplicate the "Fairyland News Mystery" worksheet and award a prize to each child who solves the mystery characters.

You can hold a fairy tale writing contest. If you do this, plan to publish the fairy tales in a book others can read in the library. Ask each author to illustrate his or her story (you can use the provided forms for both illustration and the story). If possible, have parent volunteers type the stories. The prize for these story writers could be an authors' party with cookies and punch. Try to make enough copies so that each author can receive a copy of the complete book of fairy tales. Be sure to make a title page and a table of contents with the title of each story and its author.

The original illustrations and typed stories should have a good cover (let one of the school's student artists design it) and be bound carefully so it can be a part of the library's collection. The form provided gives students a short-story starter, but be sure to let students know that they may use their own beginnings, not just the one provided.

OTHER IDEAS: _____

_____

_____

_____

_____

_____ *JANUARY ARTS AND* _____
CRAFTS CORNER

Paul Cézanne and Edouard Manet were both born in January and would make good artists to feature this month. Find some copies of some of their paintings that you can mount and exhibit along with a brief biography of each artist. Or feature illustrators of fairy tales, such as Mercer Mayer, Arthur Rackham, and others. You

THE FANTASYLAND NEWSPAPER MYSTERY

> The wicked witch of the East took her scissors and removed all of the names from the *Fantasyland News*. Can you supply the name that is missing in each news article below?

1. _____ _____ _____ _____ of 222 Woods Lane managed to escape a would-be attacker when she recognized him, even though he was disguised as a woman. She escaped into the woods and found a logger, who captured the disguised criminal.

2. _____ _____ _____ of 65 Forest Street came home to find their home had been broken into while they were away on a short walk. Nothing of value was stolen, but some food had been eaten and some furniture was upset. One item of furniture was broken. Vandals are suspected. Anyone with any information, please call the Fantasyland Police Department.

3. _____ _____, nineteen years old, has been in a coma since she was sixteen. Her parents, of 712 Spinning Wheel Lane, are hopeful that someday someone will be able to awaken their beautiful daughter.

4. _____ _____ _____, of Munchkin Place, is recovering from open-heart surgery. He has had a heart transplant and is now out of serious condition.

5. _____ _____ _____ has discovered a mysterious liquid. When you drink it, your size changes quickly. You sometimes grow and sometimes shrink to a much smaller size. Several weight-reducing salons are interested in her discovery.

_____

By _____

Once upon a time in a land far away there lived a _____

_____

_____

_____

_____

_____

_____

_____

_____

_____

_____

_____

_____

_____

_____

may be able to find publishers' posters advertising books these artists have illustrated. These posters are often beautiful and could be used on your art corner bulletin board.

For your student artist or artists of the month, ask students to bring in illustrations of their favorite fairy tale or fantasy. Remind them that the fairy tale need not be traditional—they can use modern ones such as *The Wizard of Oz,* by Frank Baum, or *The Lion, the Witch and the Wardrobe,* by C. S. Lewis. Choose one, two, or more of the best student illustrations, take a picture of each student artist, and display for all to enjoy.

OTHER IDEAS: _____

_____

_____

_____

_____

JANUARY NONFICTION CORNER

If you have been using research questions in your nonfiction corner each month, it would be nice to recognize the students who try to answer the questions. You have probably been giving small prizes to those who answer the research questions on their own, but it would be an incentive to others if you recognize the student researchers by taking their pictures and posting them somewhere in the nonfiction corner. A possible caption could be "Student Researchers."

Some questions for January's nonfiction corner are as follows:

1. On which day of the week will New Year's Day fall in 2010?
2. Who won the 1981 Super Bowl?
3. The Rose Bowl is the oldest football bowl game. In what year was it first played, and who played in it?
4. What is the mean average snowfall in Albany, New York?
5. "There is nothing so powerful as truth—and often nothing so strange" was written by a person born in January. Who?

Answers

1. Friday (See the almanac's perpetual calendar.)   2. Oakland Raiders 3. In 1902, Michigan 49, Stanford 0   4. This changes, so check your current almanac.   5. Daniel Webster (See *Bartlett's Familiar Quotations.*)

Feature biographies of famous figures born this month: Thomas Paine, Benjamin Franklin, William McKinley, Franklin Roosevelt, Martin Luther King, Jr., Joan of Arc, Louis Braille, Mozart, Richard Nixon, Robert E. Lee, Stonewall Jackson, John C. Fremont, Paul Revere, and Betsy Ross.

OTHER IDEAS: _____

_____

_____

_____

_____

_____

_____ *JANUARY SKILLS CLASSES* _____

Since all the pulled Christmas and Hanukkah books are probably still on carts waiting to be shelved, it would be good practice and a help to you for third and fourth graders to shelve the fiction and easy books and older students to shelve the nonfiction books. Get parent volunteers or your aide(s) to help, and tell students to take a book, find where it belongs on the shelf, and then raise their hands—not shelving it until you or one of your helpers checks to see that they have found the right place for it. You can have one class do all of the books (usually they like to put books away and try to see how many they can do), or you can have this as a final activity after students have finished working on an activity page. This may be less hectic, since they usually finish activity pages at different times, but you will need several classes to get all the books shelved.

In keeping with a fantasy/fairy-tale theme, some of your skills classes could deal with these genres. Ask students to list common elements of fairy tales. Discuss the differences between a fantasy and a fairy tale or a fairy tale and science fiction.

If you wish to have fairy-tale or folk-tale books pulled, or if you wish to give third and fourth graders practice using the card catalog and locating books, have them take a call slip (a set of blank slips is provided), look up the title given, write the author and the call number, and then try to find the book. Write in the titles available in your library, preferably titles in different drawers of the card catalog.

OTHER IDEAS: _____

_____

_____

_____

_____

CALL SLIPS FOR FAIRY-TALE BOOKS

Copy as many as you need. Type in the title. Ask students to look up the book in the card catalog, write in the call number and author, and then retrieve the book from the shelves.

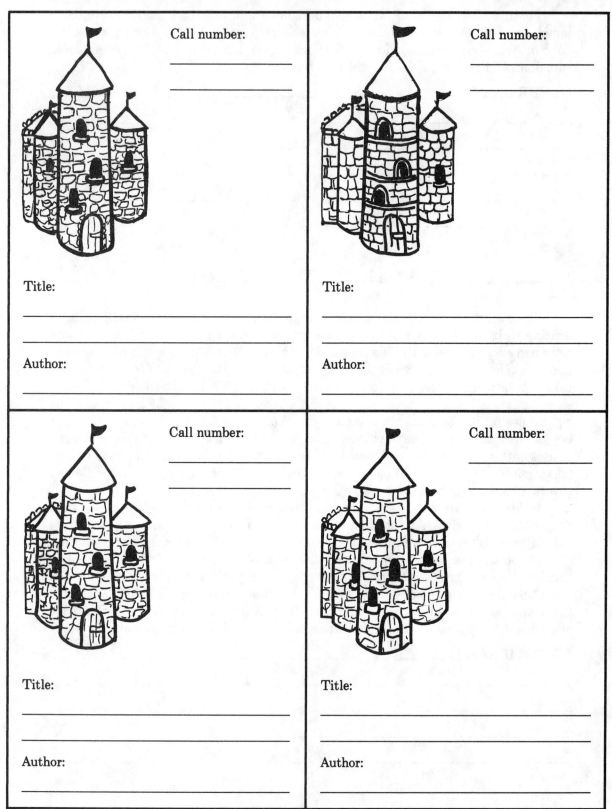

Call number:

_____

_____

Title:

_____

_____

Author:

_____

Call number:

_____

_____

Title:

_____

_____

Author:

_____

Call number:

_____

_____

Title:

_____

_____

Author:

_____

Call number:

_____

_____

Title:

_____

_____

Author:

_____

——————— *JANUARY STORYTIMES* ———————

This is the month to feature fairy tales and folk tales—traditional ones for kindergarten and first grade to be sure they are familiar with an important part of our culture, and newer or less familiar fairy tales for grades two and three. To find out which fairy tales are already familiar to students in kindergarten and first grade, use puppets and have the class tell stories such as "Little Red Riding Hood," "The Three Billy Goats Gruff," "Jack and the Beanstalk," and so on. If they are familiar with them, try the following:

Lon Po Po, translated and illustrated by Ed Young. This 1990 Caldecott Medal winner is a beautifully illustrated Chinese folk tale reminiscent of both "Little Red Riding Hood" and "The Wolf and the Seven Little Kids." In this tale, three little children outsmart a wolf who tries to masquerade as their grandmother, "Po Po." For grades one to three.

The Paperbag Princess, by Robert Munsch. A "new" fairy tale about a princess who outwits a dragon to rescue her prince, but then finds that the prince isn't quite the prince she thought he was! For grades one and two.

Princess Furball, by Charlotte Huck. This is a Cinderella-type story that also has elements of Grimm's "King Grizzly-Beard." It is well illustrated by Anita Lobel. Princess Furball runs away and finds work in the kitchen of a king. She makes such good soup that the king demands to know who the maker of the soup really is. This is for grades three and up for discussion, creative writing, and study of fairy tales.

The Principal's New Clothes, by Stephanie Calmenson. In this take-off on the familiar "The Emperor's New Clothes," a grade-school principal who is proud of his appearance is offered the most wonderful suit of all—a suit that only the best, most productive of the teachers will be able to see. This is a good springboard to creative writing for all ages.

Chicken Little, by Steven Kellogg. This retelling is a little different from the traditional "Chicken Little" story, and students in kindergarten and grade one enjoy the illustrations and dialogue.

The Three Bears and *Little Red Riding Hood,* by James Marshall. These are new versions of favorite fairy tales that children will enjoy.

The Three Sillies and *The Amazing Pig,* by Paul Galdone, are just two of this author's many popular fairy tales. Both are good for grade two.

Alexandra, the Rock-Eater, by Van Woerkam. This is a Russian fairy tale good for second and third graders. Alexandra, needing to find food for her hundred children, outwits a young dragon and his mother and comes home with many bags of gold.

What's So Funny, Ketu? and *Who's in Rabbit's House,* by Verna Aardema, are African folk tales illustrated in a colorful way that second and third graders enjoy.

Satires on fairy tales such as *Sleeping Ugly,* by Jane Yolen, and *Sidney Rella and the Glass Sneakers,* by Bernice Myers, are enjoyed by third graders. Be sure they know the real "Sleeping Beauty" story before you read *Sleeping Ugly.*

My favorite fairy tale is _____

    The best part of this fairy tale is when _____

_____

_____

_____

_____

_____

_____

My name is: _____ Grade: _____

As a change for students, use videos from PBS, such as "From the Brothers Grimm" or "Teletales," if they are still available. If not, there are many commercial fairy tales, including the popular Faerytale Theatre, now on video. Faerytale Theatre and "From the Brothers Grimm" videos can also be used with older students who can discuss plot, fairy-tale elements, and so on.

At the end of the month, or whenever you finish reading fairy tales, you might wish to have the children write about and illustrate their favorite fairy tale. An activity sheet for this is provided. Post the completed sheets in the media center, if you have room, or in the hall leading to it.

OTHER TITLES YOU LIKE:

_____

_____

_____

_____

_____

_____

JANUARY BOOK TALKS

Maintain the fairy-tale/fantasy theme in your book talks.

The Indian in the Cupboard, by Lynn Reid Banks, is a fantasy that students in grade four and up enjoy. (You will enjoy it yourself, even if fantasy is not your favorite.) Omri receives a magic white cupboard for his birthday. When he puts toys in it, they come alive. When a toy plastic Indian comes alive, Omri is at first delighted and then worried about how he will keep the tiny Indian safe and a secret. *The Return of the Indian,* a sequel to this book, will also be very popular.

Old favorites that still need to be shown to children include books such as *The White Mountains,* by John Christopher (the first book of an exciting trilogy), *The Wizard of Oz,* by L. Frank Baum, *James and the Giant Peach,* by Roald Dahl, *Chitty, Chitty, Bang, Bang,* by Ian Fleming, *The Lion, The Witch and the Wardrobe,* by C. S. Lewis, *The Book of Three,* by Lloyd Alexander, *The Trouble on Janus,* by Alfred Slote, and the many books of John Bellairs.

Using traditional and modern fairy tales can be fun with older children. Stress the traditional characteristics of a fairy tale, and then read some of the more sophisticated ones to them or use videos such as Faerytale Theatre's or PBS's "From the Brothers Grimm." Students will be surprised to find that hearing these stories when they are older is both entertaining and enlightening, for they will be able to see more of the humor and the ideas in these stories than they did when they first heard them.

The Polar Express, The Wreck of the Zephyr, and *The Mysteries of Harris Burdick* are three books by Chris Van Allsburg that are better for older children. Students have probably already heard them, but they are better suited for these sophisticated picture books now.

New fantasy and fairy-tale books are written all the time. As you find good ones, add them to the list below.

OTHER TITLES YOU LIKE: _____

_____

_____

_____

_____

_____

_____

_____

_____ *LMC MANAGEMENT* _____

Keeping in Touch with Teachers

We librarians usually have to work hard at staying in contact with the other teachers. As specialists, we sometimes feel like outsiders when the classroom teachers meet. Try to visit often with teachers, even though it takes time from the many tasks waiting to be done in the library. During lunch and before and after school, make a conscious effort to talk to them both socially and professionally to find out their needs in books and audiovisual materials.

At this time of the year we must be concerned about completing our ordering for the current year, so it is especially important to contact the classroom teachers. They can be a genuine help in suggesting orders. If you order now, the materials should come in early enough to be used this school year. Mention this at a faculty meeting, or talk to teachers on a one-to-one basis. Provide teachers with a printed form so they can list items they would like you to order. Some teachers will hand you a list, and others will never take the time to write anything down for you. Try to see these teachers personally so some grade levels will not be slighted.

If you have more requests than you have funds, order the most urgent and put the other requests in your want file. It will help you later if you get all the information about the items you place in the file: publisher or supplier, costs, order numbers, and complete address for ordering. Then, when you have funds, you can quickly order the items and remove them from the want file.

YEAR OF THE DOG

1970
1982
1994
2006

YEAR OF THE BOAR

1971
1983
1995
2007

YEAR OF THE RAT

1972
1984
1996
2008

YEAR OF THE OX

1973
1985
1997
2009

YEAR OF THE TIGER

1974
1986
1998
2010

YEAR OF THE RABBIT

1975
1987
1999
2011

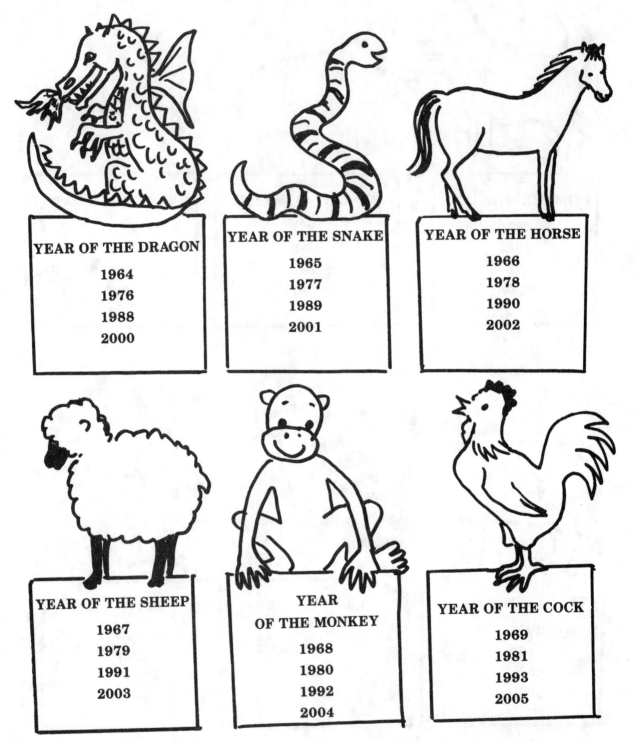

YEAR OF THE DRAGON

1964
1976
1988
2000

YEAR OF THE SNAKE

1965
1977
1989
2001

YEAR OF THE HORSE

1966
1978
1990
2002

YEAR OF THE SHEEP

1967
1979
1991
2003

YEAR
OF THE MONKEY

1968
1980
1992
2004

YEAR OF THE COCK

1969
1981
1993
2005

February

Groundhog's Day—lots of snow!
Valentine's Day and winds that blow!
Black History Month and
    Presidents Day,
Snowy fun though skies are gray!
Chinese New Year and Leap Year, too!
February's short but there's
    lots to do!

February Calendar

Snow and cold may not be as exciting now as they were in December, but there is still much to enjoy this month. Like children everywhere, we can find excitement in February with Punxatawny Phil and Groundhog Day, Valentine's Day, and Presidents Day.

February	Black History Month
February 2	Groundhog Day
February 3, 1821	Birthdate of Elizabeth Blackwell
February 3, 1894	Birthdate of Norman Rockwell
February 4, 1902	Birthdate of Charles Lindbergh
February 5, 1841	Birthdate of Pierre Auguste Renoir
February 6, 1788	Massachusetts entered the Union
February 7, 1812	Birthdate of Charles Dickens
February 8, 1910	Boy Scouts first incorporated
February 9, 1773	Birthdate of President William Henry Harrison
February 11, 1847	Birthdate of Thomas Edison
February 12, 1809	Birthdate of Abraham Lincoln
February 14	St. Valentine's Day
February 14, 1817	Birthdate of Frederick Douglass
February 14, 1859	Oregon entered the Union
February 14, 1912	Arizona entered the Union
February 15, 1820	Birthdate of Susan B. Anthony
February 22, 1732	Birthdate of George Washington
February 23, 1685	Birthdate of George Frederick Handel, composer
February 24	Mexican Flag Day
February 24, 1836	Birthdate of American artist Winslow Homer
February 27, 1807	Birthdate of Henry Wadsworth Longfellow

Check your calendar for the exact dates of

Presidents Day
Children's Dental Health Week
Chinese New Year (in January or February)
Leap Year (every four years)

_____ *FEBRUARY THEMES* _____

Since Presidents Day is in February, this is a good month for a patriotic theme such as *Know About Our Historic Past* or *Our Presidents—from Washington to Bush* (or whoever is currently president). In Canada the theme can be *Know Our Prime Ministers*. You can feature historic fiction along with these themes.

More lighthearted themes include *We Love (Your State or Province)*. Connect this theme with Valentine's Day by decorating a bulletin board with pictures from around your state or province, each highlighted with a bright "I Love You" Valentine. A theme of *We Love Books* or *We Love Authors* also fits in with Valentine's Day. In places where snow is prized for skiing, sledding, and so on, *Think Snow* is a possible theme.

Decorate the library with red, white, and blue if you use a patriotic theme (or red and white in Canada). If you choose one of the *I Love* themes, use red, pink, and white. Blue with plenty of lacy snowflakes looks good with a *Think Snow* theme.

OTHER IDEAS: _____

_____

_____

_____

_____ *SPECIAL DAYS IN FEBRUARY* _____

For Black History Month, you might want to do a special bulletin board along the lines of the one suggested in January for Martin Luther King, Jr.'s birthday. Feature a famous African American as a mystery person each week. Give one or two clues, and see how many students can name the mystery person to win a small prize. Be sure the clues allow students to solve the mystery using research skills. For example: "This African American was awarded the Nobel Prize for Peace in 1950." (Ralph Bunche) Giving something specific, like a date for a Nobel Peace Prize, allows the student to look up the information, in this case in the almanac.

Thomas Edison's birthday is a good time to display student inventions. Advertise for students to bring in any inventions, or check with teachers to see if they participate in invention activities like "INVENT America*" Many would be happy to have a place to display their students' inventions. This would also be a good day to have a speaker who is an inventor. In most cities or towns there is at least one person who has secured a patent or copyright for an invention.

_____

*U.S. Government Patent Office National Contest, Directions, Teacher & Pupil activity books.

For Mexican Flag Day, display a Mexican flag and other items from that country. If you have students of Mexican descent, perhaps they or their parents could speak to classes about Mexican customs and holidays.

For Valentine's Day, have students make a valentine for their favorite book characters. Display these on a bulletin board. Or ask students to make valentines *from* a book character. They must decide what kind of valentine their characters would send and to whom they would send it. Examples: Emily Tebbits to Otis Spofford, Curious George to the man with the yellow hat, Arthur to Francine, Tom Sawyer to Becky Thatcher, one of Miss Nelson's kids to Miss Nelson or Viola Swamp, and so on.

OTHER IDEAS: _____

_____

_____

_____

_____

FEBRUARY BULLETIN BOARDS

February's bulletin boards can be patriotic, if you have chosen a patriotic theme, or lighthearted, in keeping with Valentine's Day. For a cheerful reading incentive, display an "If the Winter is Still Here . . . " bulletin board, which features both the groundhog and a heart motif for Valentine's Day. Display book jackets on each large heart to emphasize reading. Choose book jackets about Valentine's Day or winter fun.

For the bulletin board "Read About the Presidents—from Washington to Bush" (or whoever is currently president), make your background color a bright blue or red. Cut out letters of white and stars of either red or blue, depending on the background color. A pattern for the stars is provided at the end of the previous chapter. An alternative plan: Make a large stripe each of red, white, and blue across the bulletin board. Make the letters from black, and cut the stars from gold. If you have a large bulletin board (and time and ambition), cut out enough stars for each president, writing the name of each on a star. If you have less space or time, choose as many stars as you have space for and write only the names of the most famous presidents, being sure you choose those for whom you have biographies in your library. Center a portrait of Washington and the current president in the two larger stars.

FEBRUARY AUTHORS
BIRTHDAY CLUB

What a wonderful and prolific group of authors were born in February! With Judy Blume, Laura Ingalls Wilder, and Walt Morey numbered among the authors for February, there will surely be books for anyone's taste. Jane Yolen, Norman Bridwell, and Russell Hoban are among the writers for younger children, and they, too, will be crowd pleasers. Even nonfiction lovers are well represented, with Patricia Lauber and Jill Krementz.

By now, if you have made your parties exciting, you may have more winners than you have room for in your library. This is a good time to try to have two

February Authors

February 2, 1951	Eve Rice
February 2, 1899	Rebecca Caudill
February 2, 1931	Judith Viorst
February 3, 1907	Walt Morey
February 4, 1925	Russell Hoban
February 4, 1930	Barbara Shook Hazen
February 5, 1924	Patricia Lauber
February 7, 1908	Fred Gipson
February 7, 1867	Laura Ingalls Wilder
February 8, 1838	Jules Verne
February 8, 1934	Anne Rockwell
February 9, 1908	Hilda Van Stockum
February 9, 1945	Stephen Roos
February 9, 1927	Dick Gackenbach
February 10, 1930	E. L. Konigsburg
February 11, 1939	Jane Yolen
February 12, 1945	David Small
February 12, 1938	Judy Blume
February 13, 1945	William Sleator
February 14, 1953	Paul O. Zelinsky
February 15, 1938	Norman Bridwell
February 15, 1929	Doris Orgel
February 17, 1928	Robert Peck
February 17, 1948	Susan Beth Pfeffer
February 19, 1903	Louis Slobodkin
February 19, 1940	Jill Krementz
February 21, 1936	Patricia Hermes
February 24, 1786	Wilhelm Grimm
February 23, 1932	C. S. Adler
February 25, 1914	Frank Bonham
February 25, 1942	Cynthia Voigt
February 27, 1935	Uri Shulevitz
February 27, 1919	Florence Parry Heide

WE LOVE THESE AUTHORS

WE LOVE BOOKS!

parties, splitting the group between primary and intermediate. It is easier to find a video, game, or storyteller for the group if there is not a large age spread.

On your bulletin board, write the authors for the month on hearts held by warmly dressed penguins (patterns provided). Choose only the number of authors you wish to feature, being sure you have plenty of books. If you have been having birthday club activities for several months, this would be a good time to take stock and see if the number of books required matches the students' reading skills. If not, raise or lower your expectations.

Possible sources of entertainment for your party include the middle or high school drama departments. They could perform a skit for the group, or they may know of student magicians who would welcome the chance for an audience. If your group is getting too large for cake and punch to be practical, most students enjoy something simple like ice cream bars or popcorn and apple halves.

FEBRUARY CONTEST CORNER

There are many appropriate contest possibilities for February, including the Valentine's Day and Presidents Day contests described here. Teaching magazines are also a good source of contest material.

Ask students to use any materials they like to design a clever or beautiful valentine for a favorite book character. You can give them time to do this in class, or make it a free-time contest. Post all of the valentines in the library or in the hall leading to the library. For a voluntary contest, award all participants a sticker or valentine bookmark. If you wish to judge the valentines, categories might include "Most appropriate for the character," "Prettiest," "Wittiest," "Most colorful," and so on.

A Mystery President contest is both fun and educational since it gives the students extra research practice. On a small bulletin board or on the contest board, post a heading such as "February—the Month of Presidents" with a line underneath reading, "Who Is This Mystery President?" Sample clues: "This man held the office longer than any other president. He was born in January. He was president when World War II began. Who is he?" (Franklin Roosevelt) Change the mystery president each week, first revealing the name of the previous week's president. Be sure at least one of your clues gives students a concrete piece of information they can research.

Memorize Something Patriotic

In honor of Presidents Day, offer a prize to anyone who can memorize something patriotic during the month. Have several patriotic poems or passages typed and copied so those who wish to participate can choose something to memorize. Provide shorter, easier passages for primary students. Let students come to you to recite their passage when they know it by heart. Award a small prize, and post the names of these ambitious students on a bulletin board.

It is fun for the participants and for other students in the school to have a small assembly at the end of the month to recognize the students who have memorized passages. Begin the assembly with the Pledge of Allegiance. Perhaps the music teacher can lead the group in one or two patriotic songs. Then let the students who memorized stand together and recite their passages as a group (i.e., all who memorized the Preamble to the Constitution would recite it together). Some suggestions for memorizing are as follows:

- the Preamble to the Constitution
- the Gettysburg Address
- "Hat's Off, the Flag is Passing By"
- Whitman's "Oh, Captain, My Captain"
- excerpts from "The Midnight Ride of Paul Revere"
- Emerson's "The Concord Hymn"
- Emma Lazarus's "The New Colossus" (from the base of the Statue of Liberty)
- excerpts from John F. Kennedy's "Ask not what your country can do for you" speech

You'll find many other possibilities if you ask teachers and other librarians for recommendations.

OTHER IDEAS: _____

_____

_____

_____

FEBRUARY ARTS AND CRAFTS CORNER

Decorate the corner with a computer banner or handmade banner that reads, "We Love Art!" Use cut-out red hearts to decorate your display of both famous art and student art.

Famous artists born in February include Winslow Homer, Pierre Auguste Renoir, and Norman Rockwell. All three have been featured in calendars and many other places, so you should have little difficulty finding prints of their work. Calendars are excellent sources of beautiful prints, so watch for sales of outdated calendars in bookstores and at garage sales. They will keep your art print files well supplied. All three of these artists have paintings that are interesting to children—choose one and place examples of his work and a biography of him in this month's corner.

If you are short on space, you can post the contest valentines in the art corner this month.

OTHER IDEAS: _____

_____

_____

_____

FEBRUARY NONFICTION CORNER

Two appropriate types of books to feature this month are biographies of the presidents in honor of Presidents Day and craft books that feature valentines and Valentine's Day activities (or the latter can be used in the arts and crafts corner).

If you feature presidential biographies, a red, white, and blue sign with the caption "Read About Our Presidents" would be appropriate. Then display the biographies you have available.

If you feature craft books and you do not have a plentiful supply of them, you may want to make handouts of some of the activities in the books and then keep the books on reserve in the nonfiction corner so all students may look at them.

For the February research, you might wish to have only one question a week and see how many students can find the answer. Post the names of the students who find the answer each week, and then put up a new question. Sample questions are as follows:

- Thomas Edison was born in February. Which of his many inventions is considered his greatest? (electric light)
- Elizabeth Blackwell, born February 3, 1821, is famous for what reason? (first woman doctor in the U.S.)
- Laura Ingalls Wilder, born February 7, 1867, is a famous author. What is the copyright of her book, *Little House in the Big Woods?* (1932)

Posting a question a week in the research corner rather than several for the whole month can improve participation, because students are often willing to answer one question but are not as inclined to find the answers to four or five.

OTHER IDEAS: _____

_____

_____

_____

_____

FEBRUARY SKILLS CLASSES

Finding Quotations

February provides a good time for the fifth, sixth, seventh, and eighth grades to practice using *Bartlett's Familiar Quotations.* If you haven't already introduced it to these classes, do so now, showing students how to use both the quotation index and the index to authors. Since this is an expensive book, you probably won't have many copies of it. Try, however, to have three or four copies, or borrow extra copies from another library, so you can divide the group into three or four teams. Once students find out how to use this reference book, many enjoy it. For practice, use presidential quotes or write one quotation at a time on the blackboard and let each group locate its author. Using quotations with the word *love* in them fits well with Valentine's Day. An activity page for this is provided.

Name _____ Grade _____

LOVE MAKES THE WORLD GO ROUND!

In honor of Valentine's Day, see if you can find out who said these things about love:

1. "All love is sweet,
   Given or returned."

   _____

2. "Oh, my love is like
   a red, red rose
   That's newly sprung
   in June."

   _____

3. "How do I love thee?
   Let me count the ways."

   _____

4. "It's love that makes
   the world go round."

   _____

5. "Love comforteth like
   sunshine after rain."

   _____

Usually the five quotations provided on the activity page are sufficient for a class period, but if you should need more, here are five additional quotes about love:

Men have died from time to time, and worms have eaten them, but not for love. (William Shakespeare)

So sweet love seemed that April morn, when first we kissed beside the thorn . . . (Robert Bridges)

Love is not all: it is not meat nor drink . . . (Edna St. Vincent Millay)

I was more true to Love than Love to me. (Anonymous)

Love, love, love, that is the soul of genius. (Wolfgang Amadeus Mozart)

Answers for Worksheet

1. Percy Bysshe Shelley   2. Robert Burns   3. Elizabeth Barrett Browning 4. Sir William Schwenck Gilbert   5. William Shakespeare

Research Contest

Students enjoy competition, especially in groups, so you may want to have a research contest during one library skills class. Divide your group into three or four teams (depending on the number of your reference sources). Make the groups as small as you can. Place on each table an almanac, a dictionary, a biographical dictionary, and a geographical dictionary. Ask one question at a time. The team that finds the answer first is awarded four points, the second team finished gets three points, and the other teams that find the answer in the allotted time are awarded one point each. The team with the most points wins, of course. Sample questions include the following:

1. Are there any cities named Valentine, and, if so, where are they?
2. When did St. Valentine live?
3. Who said, "See, Winter comes to rule the varied year, sullen and sad?"
4. What is a "love apple"?
5. On which day of the week will Valentine's Day fall in the year 2010?

Answers

1. Valentine, Nebraska   2. third century   3. James Thomson in "The Seasons"   4. a tomato   5. Sunday

There is usually time for five to ten questions, depending on the group. This game is a great favorite, but try to ensure that groups are evenly matched in ability. You may need to specify that each student in the group is to take a turn

FEBRUARY CALL NUMBER SLIPS

Look up books appropriate for February. Write the call number in the upper corner of each card and the title in the valentine carried by each penguin.

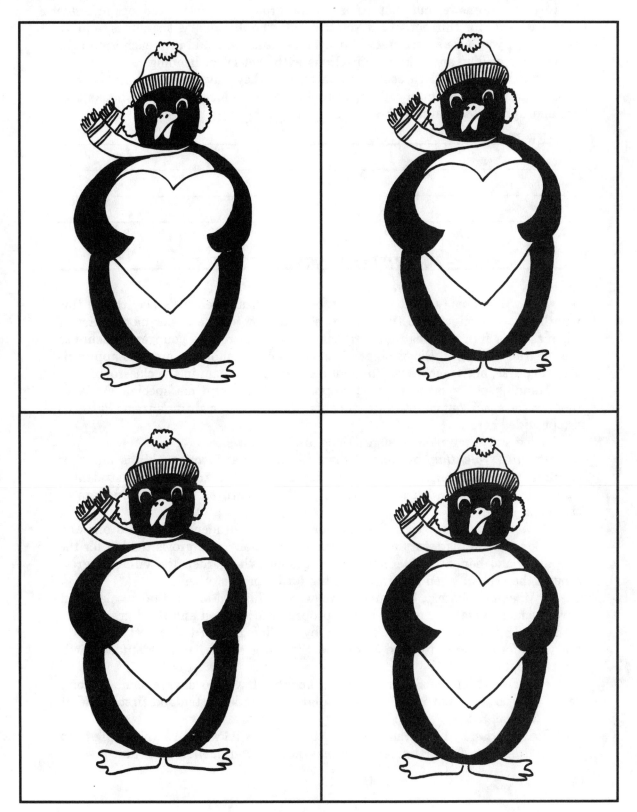

looking up the answer but that others in the group may help. Students in grade four are ready for this activity if you use only the dictionary, thesaurus, and an almanac. If you have several sets of encyclopedias, you could give each group the same letter volume and ask only questions with that letter heading.

Students in grade three (or grade two, if they have been taught location skills) can use the penguin call slips provided here to locate and pull books that are appropriate to showcase this month.

OTHER IDEAS: _____

_____

_____

_____

FEBRUARY STORYTIMES

You will probably want to feature books with a Valentine's Day theme this month, but you might also find it fun to read some of the easier biographies of Thomas Edison or Charles Lindbergh and thereby introduce younger students to the biography section. Biographies of Lincoln and Washington are also appropriate, of course, but teachers will undoubtedly be using them in the classroom.

Handing out snowman finger puppets makes storytime special. Or leave them at the check-out counter for students to take as a Valentine's treat. Patterns are provided here.

Some storytime reading suggestions are as follows:

Arthur's Valentine, by Marc Brown. A perennial favorite, this is one that children never tire of. After the story, it might be fun to give each student a candy heart printed with a message, like those featured on the endpapers of the book.

A Sweetheart for a Valentine, by Lorna Balian. Students in grades one and two enjoy this fantasy story about a little orphan baby who grows too big for the people around her. Students enjoy hearing about the garden the villagers grow around the orphan when she grows too big for them to clothe.

A Valentine Fantasy, by Carolyn Haywood. This is a modern fairy tale about how Valentine's Day began, and it is appropriate for second and third graders.

The Lady with the Alligator Purse, by Nadine Bernard Westcott. This is a great one for kindergarten and grade one. Sing it or read it, and the students will want to join in!

Pierre, by Maurice Sendak. This is about a boy who always said, "I don't care!" It is not new, but it is always popular with kindergarten and first grade. It is fun to read, too!

Pig Surprise, by Ute Krause. For her birthday, Nina wanted a guinea pig from her Aunt Agatha. Unfortunately, she was not a good speller and Aunt Agatha

FINGER PUPPET PATTERNS

thought Nina wanted a "genuine" pig. So she sends Nina a genuine pig, named Herman, who tries his best to be a "house pig." For grades one through three.

OTHER TITLES YOU LIKE: _____

_____

_____

_____

_____

_____ *FEBRUARY BOOK TALKS* _____

At the beginning of the month, introduce the authors featured in the authors birthday club in your book talks. Have other books by these authors available to show students. Sound filmstrips or videos are available for many of the books by Judy Blume and by Laura Ingalls Wilder, two of the February authors.

Volcano, by Patricia Lauber. Some of the students may not have participated in the authors book club because most of the books featured have been fiction. This and many other of Patricia Lauber's nonfiction books may interest these students. Her books are well written and readable.

Soup, by Robert Peck. This is a good one to feature because after you have interested the class in the adventures of Soup, you can show them many books about this enterprising character. Written in the first person, the author tells how Soup constantly gets him into trouble. These books are readable and fun for students in grades four to six, and even for some third graders.

The Great Brain, by John D. Fitzgerald. This can be discussed with *Soup* since the title character in both series is a manipulator and a sometime con man. Again, there are many Great Brain books, so there will be plenty for students to choose from.

Number the Stars, by Lois Lowry. This 1990 Newbery winner is easy to read and yet interesting enough to read to students. It is based on the Danish effort during World War II to rescue the Jews in Denmark by sneaking them by boat to Sweden. How Annemarie and her family help save her best friend Ellen and her family is an engrossing story, especially since it is based on an actual happening.

OTHER TITLES YOU LIKE: _____

_____

_____

_____

_____

—————————— *LMC MANAGEMENT* ——————————

Card Filing

If you are not lucky enough to have a computerized card catalog, you are probably swamped with unfiled catalog cards by this time of the year. While the catalog would probably be more meticulously accurate if you filed all the cards yourself, there is just not enough time for the typical teaching librarian to do this. A trained volunteer is one solution, but train only one or two volunteers, and train them well. You can make a chart of the most puzzling card catalog rules, such as "Dr." being filed as "doctor" and "Mrs." as "mistress." You may have a few cards misfiled, but that can happen in any case.

You may be fortunate enough to have paid library assistants who can be trained to file catalog and shelf cards and leave you free to concentrate on teaching, library reading programs, and your many other duties.

Another plan is to have some of your classes to do the filing as part of their study of the card catalog. In this case, give each student a catalog drawer and a stack of cards to be filed in that drawer. Do not let students remove the rod from the drawer; ask them to set the cards in the proper place on the rod. When they raise their hands to indicate that their cards are completed, you can quickly check to see if they have filed them correctly. If so, remove the rod and secure the cards. Students who are finished can use the remaining class time to browse, look at magazines, or help other students.

In any case, do not let these catalog cards pile up, or you will find yourself spending long hours filing at the end of the year or even carrying filing over to the next year.

Weeding

You may plan to do extensive weeding while taking inventory, but during the year weed any books that appear to be beyond repair, have become factually outdated, or are offensively biased. What to do with weeded books is a problem. Some school districts have their own policy for how to dispose of these books. If a book is offensive or inaccurate, it is best to destroy it. If the book is merely too worn for circulation but has reading life, most librarians hate to destroy it. Some schools allow a used book fair at the end of the year, when these books can be sold for a minimal amount. If you choose to do this, be sure the book is stamped in some way so it will not inadvertently return to your shelves. Remove the card and card pocket and ink out your library name wherever it appears. Stamp the book "Withdrawn." Some librarians like to compose their own stamp for use with such books, something like, "This book has been read and loved by the students of _____ School. Make it a friend." You can have a stamp made that fits your particular needs.

If you must dispose of some books, be sure to do this in an inconspicuous place. It is not good public relations if people see books being thrown out; some will not understand it even if the book is practically in shreds. Remove the cards and card pockets and ink out the school name on these books. Some libraries remove the covers.

Be sure to remove the shelf and catalog cards of withdrawn books from your files. Subject cards are especially important, so first remove the shelf card and then trace your subject cards from it. Library assistants can be trained to do the pulling of the cards and the preparation of books for disposal, but you should be responsible for the weeding.

March

Windy, wild, and stormy days,
Then sunny light through shadow plays!
Cold, then warm; winter, then spring,
No one knows what each day will bring!
Will the weather be cruel or will it be kind?
March never seems to make up its mind!

March Calendar

March is a turning point—winter is ending and spring is beginning. In the school year, too, March signals the beginning of the end: so much to do and so little time left before the summer break!

March	Red Cross Month
March 1, 1803	Ohio entered the Union
March 1, 1867	Nebraska entered the Union
March 3, 1847	Birthdate of Alexander Graham Bell
March 3, 1845	Florida entered the Union
March 3, 1931	"The Star Spangled Banner" became the national anthem
March 4, 1791	Vermont entered the Union
March 5, 1770	Anniversary of the Boston Massacre
March 6, 1475	Birthdate of Michelangelo
March 6, 1836	Alamo Day
March 12, 1912	Girl Scouts founded
March 14, 1879	Birthdate of Albert Einstein
March 15, 1767	Birthdate of President Andrew Jackson
March 15, 1820	Maine entered the Union
March 16, 1751	Birthdate of President James Madison
March 17	St. Patrick's Day
March 18, 1837	Birthdate of President Grover Cleveland
March 18, 1959	Hawaii became the forty-ninth state
March 19, 1903	Birthdate of Lou Gehrig
March 22, 1846	Birthdate of Randolph Caldecott
March 26, 1874	Birthdate of poet Robert Frost
March 26, 1930	Birthdate of Justice Sandra Day O'Connor
March 29, 1790	Birthdate of President John Tyler
March 30, 1853	Birthdate of Vincent Van Gogh

Check your calendar for exact dates of

National Wildlife Week
First day of spring
Girl Scout Week

MARCH THEMES

One of the most popular and prolific children's authors has a birthday in March—Theodore Geisel, better known as Dr. Seuss. An appropriate theme would be *Dr. Seuss Month.* The Cat in the Hat, Sam-I-Am, and Horton the Elephant can all be found as stuffed animals, and you could feature these in a prominent place. Primary storytimes could feature some of the many books by Dr. Seuss. Older children could try to write a book in the rhyming style of Dr. Seuss. Bulletin boards could advertise his many books.

Another possible theme could be *Dinosaur Daze.* You can use many commercially produced items with this theme, including model dinosaurs, large, floor-sized puzzles of dinosaurs, dinosaur games, etc. Bulletin boards can feature dinosaurs and contests and research questions about these prehistoric animals. Bookmarks and posters are available from library supply companies like Upstart (see Appendix). Students in the primary grades seem to be the most interested in dinosaurs, but even upper-grade students will enjoy the research and the many audiovisual items available on dinosaurs.

OTHER IDEAS: _____

_____

_____

_____

_____

SPECIAL DAYS IN MARCH

Several states entered the Union in March: Nebraska, Ohio, Florida, Vermont, Maine, and Hawaii all became states this month. On the day of each state's admittance, post questions about it on a sign at the check-out desk. Give a small prize to all students who are able to answer the questions. For instance, on the day of Nebraska's statehood, you could post the following:

Nebraska became a state on March 1, 1867.

Do you know the answers to these questions about Nebraska?

1. What is the capital city of Nebraska?
2. What is the state bird of Nebraska?
3. What is the state flower of Nebraska?
4. What state is found to the east of Nebraska?

Answers

1. Lincoln   2. Meadowlark   3. Goldenrod   4. Iowa

Ask as many questions as you feel appropriate. Do the same for each state achieving statehood in March. (Ohio entered the Union on March 1 also, so you may want to choose between Ohio and Nebraska or delay the questions for one state by one day.)

In honor of the birthdate of Alexander Graham Bell on March 3, 1847, have an Alexander Graham Bell Day. Try to bring in examples of telephones—if possible, a range of them from the earliest to the latest. Your telephone company may be willing to provide an exhibit and someone to talk to the students about telephones and telephone usage. You might ask a teacher to have a group of interested students prepare a panel discussion of how the world has been changed by the telephone. The panel could talk to some of the library classes.

OTHER IDEAS: _____

_____

_____

_____

_____

_____

_____

_____

_____

_____ *MARCH BULLETIN BOARDS* _____

Both bulletin board suggestions for this month fit the theme of *Dinosaur Daze*. The first, "Did the Dinosaurs Die Out Because They Couldn't Read?" can be discussed in some of your classes. Ask students to tell you various reasons scientists give for the end of the dinosaurs. If you have access to a science museum representative or a paleontologist, invite him or her to come and talk to the classes about dinosaurs and the scientific theories of their demise.

"What's Wrong with This Picture?" can promote student participation, as students try to tell you what is wrong. (The answer, of course, is that there were no humans at the time of the dinosaurs.)

Make the backgrounds of each board pale green, with lavendar mountains, brown rocks, and bright blue skies.

MARCH AUTHORS
BIRTHDAY CLUB

If you have had a blue or red background for your authors birthday club bulletin board, you may wish to change it this month to something more spring-like. A yellow background with kelly green or blue letters would be appropriate, or perhaps a sky-blue background with letters of yellow or green. In any case, decide on the authors you wish to feature this month and place their names on shamrocks; then arrange them around the birthday cake. (Patterns are provided at the end of this chapter.)

If you have a large number of birthday club readers this month and you would like to try something easier than birthday cake and punch, a build-your-own-sundae party is fun. You need a gallon or two of ice cream and several flavors of toppings. Give students a scoop of ice cream and let them add the toppings. If time permits, a *Robin Hood* movie (in honor of Howard Pyle, born March 5, 1853) or a movie or video of *Black Beauty,* in honor of Anna Sewell, would be appropriate entertainment. If you are having separate parties for primary and intermediate grades, you will be able to find many different movies or videos of books by Dr. Seuss for the primary grades.

If you can find several sets of the game Authors, students might enjoy this instead of a video. Also be on the lookout for local storytellers, puppeteers, and magicians.

OTHER IDEAS: _____

_____

_____

_____

MARCH CONTEST CORNER

Because St. Patrick's Day is this month, students might enjoy a "Finding of the Green" contest. Give a prize to the student in each grade who can find the most titles of books in the library that either contain the word *green* or whose author's last name is Green or Greene.

Somewhere in the contest corner, post a weekly mystery character from Dr. Seuss. Since Dr. Seuss characters are so familiar, the riddles need to be a little more subtle than most of the contest corner riddles. Encourage thesaurus or dictionary use by using difficult words in your riddles; for example, a riddle about Yertle, the Turtle, could say, "This amphibian was a braggart who wished to be monarch of all he could survey." For Horton the Elephant: "This pachyderm was duped by an indolent bird." Most students enjoy riddles and will go to great lengths to answer them. A Dr. Seuss bookmark would make a good prize for the weekly winners.

March Authors

March 2, 1904	Theodore Geisel (Dr. Seuss)
March 2, 1921	Helen Sattler
March 3, 1938	Patricia MacLachlan
March 4, 1906	Meindert DeJong
March 5, 1946	Mem Fox
March 5, 1853	Howard Pyle
March 6, 1949	Thatcher Hurd
March 8, 1859	Kenneth Grahame
March 10, 1920	Jack Kent
March 11, 1893	Wanda Gag
March 12, 1936	Daniel Cohen
March 12, 1936	Virginia Hamilton
March 13, 1928	Ellen Raskin
March 13, 1933	Thomas Rockwell
March 14, 1889	Marguerite DeAngeli
March 15, 1932	Barbara Cohen
March 16, 1920	Sid Fleischman
March 20, 1942	Ellen Conford
March 20, 1937	Lois Lowry
March 23, 1912	Eleanor Cameron
March 24, 1920	Mary Stolz
March 27, 1922	Dick King Smith
March 30, 1820	Anna Sewell

Don't forget to look in magazines like *Challenge* and *Creative Kids* for suitable contests. Keep a monthly file of suitable library contests.

OTHER IDEAS: _____

_____

_____

_____

_____

MARCH ARTS AND CRAFTS CORNER

Continue to encourage student artists to submit their work so you can change this feature of the art corner often.

Michelangelo, one of the world's most famous artists, was born in March, so an exhibit of some prints of his work along with a brief biography would be appropriate.

With March's windy weather, craft books on making kites, paper airplanes, model rockets, and so on would be welcome. Encourage students to design their own kites and display them in this corner. These designs can either be actual kites or colored drawings of kites. Or, rather than having students make the kites, you can display different kinds of kites along with the crafts books—box kites, Japanese fish kites, and other types of kites make a colorful exhibit.

If there are teachers or staff in your school who are talented in arts and crafts, ask them if you can display their work in this corner. Be sure to post their photo and a brief biography next to their work.

OTHER IDEAS: _____

_____

_____

_____

MARCH NONFICTION CORNER

Since Albert Einstein's birthday is in March, you could feature biographies of geniuses (including Alexander Graham Bell), or focus on inventors or scientists. If you find that your list needs some minority or female representatives, consider George Washington Carver, Benjamin Banneker, Marie Curie, Barbara McClintock, and Margaret Mead.

Post research questions (one each week or four all at once) on a small bulletin board in this corner. Possible questions include the following:

1. Which became a state first, Ohio or Maine?
2. What is Florida's state flower?
3. Alexander Graham Bell was born March 3, 1847. He invented the telephone. Where was he born?
4. On what day of the week will St. Patrick's Day be celebrated in the year 2010?
5. Randolph Caldecott, a famous illustrator of children's books, was born March 22, 1846. When was the Caldecott Medal for best illustrated children's book first awarded?

Answers

1. Ohio, in 1803 2. orange blossom 3. Edinburgh, Scotland 4. Wednesday 5. for the year 1938

OTHER IDEAS: _____

_____

_____

_____

_____

——————— *MARCH SKILLS CLASSES* ———————

Publishing Books

Publishing books with students, ideally in grade three, is an excellent way to help them learn about books, the library, and shelving.

If possible, have the students write and illustrate their books in the classroom. This will, of course, involve the third-grade teachers, so you will have to enlist their help several weeks before the planned library classes. Students' books can be written during library classes, but this will take a great deal of time that would be better spent on library skills.

After the books are written and illustrated, assemble them. For each book, you will need two railroad board covers (on which you can glue an illustration made by the student), three blank pages before the beginning of the text and one at the end. A blank call number tag should be placed on the spine and a card pocket and card on the inside of the cover. Bind the books in the best method you have available.

On the first day of publishing, discuss with the students what a good cover should have on it. After students come to the conclusion that a cover needs the title of the book, author, and illustrator and a picture, let each student check to see if his or her book has these elements. Then have students open their books, and discuss with them why most books have blank endpapers or cover sheets. Elicit from students ideas such as "to protect the important part of the book" (you can tell them this is called the text) or "it gives you a place to write the name of the book's owner." This is probably all the time you will have. Encourage students to look at the books they check out to see if they have good covers and cover pages.

Use the next session to have students make their own title pages. Provide library books with good title pages so students can look at them and list the elements on them: title, author, illustrator, publisher, and place published. Then have each student make a title page for his or her own book. As the place published, use the name of the town the school is in. Let each student make up a name for the publishing company, after you discuss together what a publisher does: buy books from authors, edit them, print them, and sell them. Students will see that they themselves, their teacher, and you have all worked as publishers for their books. Give them a few suggestions, such as "Library Publishing Company" or "_____ School Press." Tell them they can make up their own name, something like "Peanutbutter Press" or "Lollipop Publishing Co." As students finish their title pages, check them and then let students browse and check out books.

On the third day of publishing, discuss copyright and why the author needs a copyright. Then discuss how the copyright date can help readers to be sure the material is not dated. Have them find the copyright date on an actual book and then discuss the usual location of the copyright date. Then have students put a copyright date on the back of the title page of their own books.

Don't forget to review each day what has previously been taught. Since the time allotted for teaching skills varies with each librarian, you may be able to proceed faster or may have to go slower than suggested here.

The next step is to discuss the book's dedication and let the children put a dedication in their own books. Discuss as well the table of contents, index, and glossary, terms students will probably know from their reading classes. Explain that these are not needed in their books because they are short. Discuss the card and card pocket and how they are used. Then make a card and card pocket that match. You may want them to write "PB" and the date in the right-hand corner so these cards will not get mixed up with the regular cards. Write a call number on the outside of students' books. Then let students find the place in the library where their books should be located.

Students enjoy leaving their books in the library for other students to check out. In some schools, these books are left in the library until the students are in the last grade of the school. If your library is computerized, you will need to decide whether you want to put a bar code on these student-produced books. Producing student books does involve some expense, but it is worth it because of student involvement and learning.

When the books are complete and students have found where they belong on the shelves, let each student be the first to check his or her book out. In the following weeks, students can practice shelving books and locating books using these call numbers and titles. With some groups you may wish to go on to making sample catalog cards for the books they have made, or you may prefer to save this activity for fourth-grade classes.

OTHER IDEAS: _____

_____

_____

_____

MARCH STORYTIMES

Some teachers do not like to read Dr. Seuss stories aloud because of their insistent and often tongue-tying rhyming, but some of his stories are great for storytimes and students in kindergarten through grade two really enjoy them. Some of the best for reading aloud are listed here.

Horton Hatches the Egg. Everyone is happy that Horton, the faithful, who has sat on the nest of Lazy Maisie for so long, should be rewarded with an elephant-bird! There are Horton stuffed toys available; if you have one, show it before the story and let the students take turns holding it. Another prestory activity is to hide a small toy elephant in a box and let students play Twenty Questions to see if they can guess the animal in the box. (Don't show the book you are going to read first—they'll figure it out too quickly!)

The Sneetches. Students also like this story of the "Star-Belly Sneetches" who resented and snubbed Sneetches without stars. Giving the students a star with something printed on it such as "I'm Somebody!" might be appropriate and help build self-esteem.

Yertle the Turtle. Students both understand and enjoy this story of Yertle, who thinks he is king of the pond but finally learns that he is only king as long as the turtles beneath him let him be king. A good prestory activity for this is to have the students learn Vachel Lindsay's "The Little Turtle." Don't forget the actions of crawling on the grass and crawling on the rocks (crawl fingers across your arms and hands). The children enjoy it when you pretend to "snap at a mosquito" and then snap "at me."

The Butter Battle Book. Students in grade three enjoy this. After reading the story, ask them if they think they know what Dr. Seuss was trying to say.

McElligot's Pool. This is a story about all the fish that were found in McElligot's pool. If you have time, give each first grader a piece of paper. Have students go to tables where crayons or felt-tip pens are available and draw and color a picture of what they caught in McElligot's pool. These can make a colorful, effective bulletin board.

To wrap up these Dr. Seuss readings, take a poll to determine which is the school's favorite Dr. Seuss story. Graph the results and post them somewhere in the library.

Other books to feature this month include Jack Kent's, which are always fun to read aloud. Some of his best are *Joey, Silly Goose* (a great one!), and *Fat Cat.* Another birthday author, Mem Fox, wrote *Night Noises,* which first and second graders enjoy. Lily Laceby is nearly ninety and lives by herself with her dog, Butch. One winter evening she dreams of things she had done long ago. As she sleeps, noises begin in the night—a knocking, crackling, and finally a pounding. Who could be outside her house on such a night?

OTHER TITLES YOU LIKE: _____

_____

_____

_____

_____

_____

MARCH BOOK TALKS

Sometimes it seems that there is not enough time for book talks, with all the library skills that need to be taught. Taking one week a month to do book talks, however, is rewarding, for it stimulates and diversifies the students' reading, which often is focused on just one kind of book—mysteries, certain kinds of nonfiction, Babysitter Club books, and so on. Using the first week of the month to do these book talks will also enable you to remind students of the authors birthday club and to accent the authors who are represented that month. Some of the delightful books written by March authors include the following:

How to Eat Fried Worms, by Thomas Rockwell. You might want to introduce this book by showing students some of the strange foods that people eat. Visit a specialty food store and bring back some chocolate-covered grasshoppers or another strange food. Then ask, "How would you like to eat fried worms?" If you prefer, there are audiovisual presentations of this story, but sometimes the book talk is more effective.

Anastasia on Her Own, by Lois Lowry. This is one of Lowry's many entertaining books. Anastasia frequently complains that her mother is an inefficient housekeeper, so her mother leaves her in charge of the household when she is called away on business. The results are funny and at times disastrous.

The One Hundredth Thing About Caroline, also by Lois Lowry. This is an especially good book to feature this month if you have chosen dinosaurs as a theme.

Caroline wants to be a paleontologist, so she studies dinosaurs at every opportunity. She and her best friend Stacy discover what they think is a plot to kill Caroline and her brother, and their efforts to solve the mystery and thwart the plot make this an entertaining book. You can introduce this by showing a model of a stegosaurus and asking students if they know the name of this dinosaur. It is Caroline's favorite dinosaur and can lead into the story.

Me and the Terrible Two, by Ellen Conford. Dorrie's best friend moves away, and two twin boys move in next door. Dorrie is heart-broken that her friend is gone, and now she believes that the twins are purposely trying to tease and torture her. After talking about this book, show some of Conford's other popular books.

The House of Dies Drear, by Virginia Hamilton. Popular with students, this is a good book to recommend to teachers for reading aloud. Then students will come in wanting to read it on their own. This book is available in video and sound filmstrip.

For the nonfiction enthusiasts, Daniel Cohen, a featured March author, has many popular nonfiction books you can show the classes.

OTHER TITLES YOU LIKE: _____

_____

_____

_____

_____

_____

_____

_____

_____ *LMC MANAGEMENT* _____

Book Fairs

Book fairs are becoming an important source of income for school librarians, whose budgets are often cut or made less effective by rising book costs.

A list of book fair companies is given in the Appendix. These are commercial distributors of book fairs, but you may also find local book stores or paperback jobbers who will give you a good discount if you use their books for a book fair. The advantage of using local companies is that you can visit the store or jobber and select the books particularly suited to the students in your school. If you use a commercial distributor, usually you must take the books they bring.

There are, however, some distinct advantages to using commercial book fairs. Convenience is a major advantage. The companies supply advertising, including flyers that list the books to be sold, banners to post in your school, and often sample letters to send home to parents. The books come arranged in cases that need only be opened. At night or when the fair is over, these cases are closed and locked—you won't have to unpack boxes or try to figure out where the books can be displayed. The companies also supply worksheets for figuring out your sales and discounts, and their discounts in both cash and free books are usually better than a bookstore or jobber can afford to offer.

Planning Ahead

You can schedule a book fair anytime, so choose a time that fits your school's schedule. Because of National Children's Book Week in November and National Library Week in April, these two months are good choices. However, you can sometimes get a better commission in cash and free books if you schedule your fair in a less popular month, like February. February is also a good time because some parents will buy books for their children for Valentine's Day.

Whatever time you choose, schedule as far in advance as possible so you can be sure of getting the time you want. Plan on holding the fair for approximately five school days, since this is the amount of time most companies allow.

At least two weeks before your scheduled fair, secure parent volunteers who can be in the book fair area during lunch and after school. If you have plenty of volunteers, it is also helpful to have the entire school day covered, since you and your aide will also have regular library duties to attend to. If you cannot get enough volunteers, you will need to be in the book fair area during regularly scheduled library classes.

The day before the fair is to begin, get enough money so you can make change during the first hours of the sale. Decide where the money will be kept each night after the fair is closed. Try to place the fair in a corner of the media center or in a comparatively enclosed area so you can watch out for students taking books without paying for them. Most commercial companies do not hold you responsible for stolen books, but you want to reduce temptation as much as possible.

Book fairs take time, but the money earned from them can be used to pay for a visit from a storyteller or author. The free books usually given to the library as part of the commission for having the fair can be used for prizes for the authors book club parties or for other library contests. In the age of declining budgets and escalating costs, the school book fair is a worthwhile endeavor.

April

April rain and April sun
Show spring is here and winter's done!
Skateboards, bikes, and jump-ropes tell
That we are under springtime's spell!

April Calendar

You can plan many exciting activities relating to National Library Week. Because the end of the school year is drawing near, plan something fun for this special week.

April	Keep America Beautiful Month
April	National Sense of Humor Month
April 1	April Fool's Day
April 2	International Children's Book Day (in honor of Hans Christian Andersen)
April 9, 1865	Lee surrendered to Grant
April 12, 1861	Civil War began with firing on Fort Sumter
April 13, 1743	Birthdate of President Thomas Jefferson
April 14, 1866	Birthdate of Anne Sullivan
April 15	Tax Day
April 15, 1452	Birthdate of Leonardo da Vinci
April 18, 1775	Paul Revere's famous ride
April 19, 1775	Patriot's Day commemorates battles of Lexington and Concord
April 23, 1923	Birthdate of President James Buchanan
April 26, 1785	Birthdate of John James Audubon
April 26, 1822	Birthdate of President Ulysses S. Grant
April 28, 1758	Birthdate of President James Monroe
April 28, 1788	Maryland entered the Union
April 30, 1812	Louisiana entered the Union

Check your calendar for the exact dates of

Arbor Day (varies from state to state)
National Library Week
Easter
Passover
Earth Day/Earth Week

© 1991 by The Center for Applied Research in Education

_____ *APRIL THEMES* _____

With National Library Week in April, most of the themes suggested here focus on books or on reading. Some possible themes include *Read—It Becomes You!*, *Begin a Lifetime of Fun—Read!*, *Those Who Read Get Ahead!*, and *Reading Is a Good Habit*. Other possible themes include *Beverly Cleary Month*, since April is her birthday month, and *Our Wonderful World*, since April is Keep America Beautiful Month and contains Arbor Day and Earth Day as well. James Audubon's April birthday could provide the theme, *April—It's for the Birds*. Bulletin boards and featured books should relate to your theme.

To play up a bird theme, feature posters of birds, books about them, and bulletin boards featuring books and birds. Try to get a birdwatcher or a member of the Audubon Society to come to the library and talk to students. Perhaps a parent or a pet shop would loan your library a parakeet or some other bird for the month.

For the *Our Wonderful World* theme, feature books about some of the world's beautiful places, as well as both fiction and nonfiction books from other countries as well as our own. Books that focus on ecology would also fit in well here.

A *Beverly Cleary Month* can be lots of fun, with characters like Ramona, Henry Huggins, and Ralph the Mouse to brighten the bulletin boards and walls.

OTHER IDEAS: _____

_____

_____

_____

_____ *SPECIAL DAYS IN APRIL* _____

Since April is National Sense of Humor Month, students would undoubtedly enjoy having one day set aside as the School Library Joke Day. On that day, let students tell jokes they have read in one of the library's joke and riddle books. Give a bookmark or sticker to each joke teller.

Other dates you might feature are the statehood days of Maryland and Louisiana, or Thomas Jefferson's birthday. Jefferson was one of our most distinguished and versatile presidents, which makes it easy to think of good questions to ask students. Post his picture and challenge students to answer questions like, "Thomas Jefferson was an architect. What is one thing he designed?" and "Thomas Jefferson was an author. Name one thing he wrote."

OTHER IDEAS: _____

_____

_____

_____

APRIL BULLETIN BOARDS

Two suggestions for April bulletin boards are "April—It's for the Birds! Read About Them!" and "Fly High with Books!" The first fits well into a bird theme centered around the birthday of Audubon. Use a blue background, and color the bird either as a robin or as another favorite bird. Cut the nest from light brown construction paper, and glue dried grass to it for a special effect. Make the branch of the tree a darker brown.

The balloon in "Fly High with Books" should be as colorful as possible. Cut the stripes from bright colors of construction paper, or color the stripes with felt-tip pens. Use string for the lines attaching the balloon to its basket and, if possible, use actual book covers in the children's hands. Patterns for both boards are provided at the end of this chapter.

APRIL AUTHORS
BIRTHDAY CLUB

April's authors include some real child pleasers such as Patricia Reilly Giff, Ruth Chew, Marguerite Henry, and, of course, the popular and prolific Beverly Cleary. Barbara Park and Lois Duncan are popular authors for fourth through seventh grade. There is a wide range of reading levels among these authors. Ruth Chew's books are good for students just beginning to read something other than

April Authors

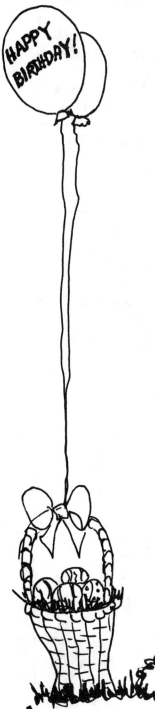

April 1, 1926	Anne McCaffrey
April 2, 1805	Hans Christian Andersen
April 4, 1932	Johanna Reiss
April 4, 1943	Elizabeth Levy
April 5, 1934	Richard Peck
April 8, 1920	Ruth Chew
April 10, 1947	David Adler
April 10, 1903	Clare Newberry
April 12, 1911	Barbara Corcoran
April 12, 1916	Beverly Cleary
April 12, 1907	Hardie Gramatky
April 13, 1938	Lee Bennett Hopkins
April 13, 1902	Marguerite Henry
April 14, 1927	Robert Lopshire
April 16, 1922	John Christopher
April 24, 1911	Evaline Ness
April 25, 1927	Alvin Schwartz
April 25, 1933	Larry Kettelkamp
April 26, 1937	Patricia Reilly Giff
April 27, 1924	Roy Gallant
April 27, 1947	Barbara Park
April 28, 1934	Lois Duncan
April 30, 1892	Maria Leach

picture books, and the more difficult books by Johanna Reiss, Anne McCaffrey, and Richard Peck are suitable for more advanced readers. Larry Kettelkamp and Alvin Schwartz are among several nonfiction authors who will be able to satisfy the nonfiction lovers. Present the books and their authors enthusiastically, stressing that there is something suitable for everyone, and your birthday club party should be the biggest ever.

You will find the rabbits for this month's festive bulletin board at the end of this chapter.

A special activity for this month could be the launching of helium-filled balloons by all of the authors birthday club participants. Have each child write his or her name and address on a card bearing the message, "I am a member of the Authors Birthday Club of _____ Library. If you find my balloon, please write to me." (You may prefer to have students use the school address.) If you can do this ahead of time, laminate the cards; otherwise, place them in small plastic bags and attach each to a balloon. Children can launch their balloons from the playground or another open area. It is a more effective sight if they are all released at once, on your signal. After this, the students can return to the library for their treats.

You can purchase helium in tanks. Sometimes companies that sell helium will fill the balloons free if they know you are from a school. Sometimes parent volunteers will agree to fill the balloons for you. Don't fill the balloons with helium until the day of the launch, since helium will escape quickly, especially in hot weather.

Ask students to bring in any cards that are returned so the places where balloons were found can be posted in the library. Take pictures of the colorful launch and post them on your bulletin board.

OTHER IDEAS: _____

_____

_____

_____

_____ *APRIL CONTEST CORNER* _____

If you didn't use the scavenger hunt provided in September, this would be a good month to use it, since it acquaints students with the library during National Library Week. If you already used the scavenger hunt, you might ask students to use it in the public library. Give each student who completes it a small prize.

Students love a contest with an art activity. Try copying a complicated geometric design and challenging students to color it. You will be surprised at the different designs and color combinations students will create. You can award small prizes for "Boldest," "Most Colors Used," "Most Unusual," "Neatest," and so on. Posting the artwork in the library makes a colorful display in the art corner or the contest corner.

OTHER IDEAS: _____

_____

_____

_____

APRIL ARTS AND CRAFTS CORNER

Since this month includes National Library Week, it would be a good month to ask children to illustrate a favorite story. Display the illustrations in the art corner. To make the corner very attractive, mat the illustrations and include the name of the book illustrated, the name of the student, and a photograph of the student. If you cannot afford film for a picture of each student contributing an illustration, ask him or her to bring in a photo.

When you announce this contest, give the students some guidelines. For example, the illustration must be their own, not copied from a book. Tell them the size of the paper they are to use, and offer some suggestions on media. Encourage them to use color, from crayons, felt-tip pens, cut construction paper, etc. You might show them some examples of illustrations using these different media. If you have time in your library classes, you could get students started, but since your time is probably filled with skills activities, you might ask teachers to use an art period for book illustrations. You could then select some for the art corner and others for the hall or classrooms.

OTHER IDEAS: _____

_____

_____

_____

APRIL NONFICTION CORNER

If you have chosen birds for your theme for April, display books about birds. Hang posters of birds. Display birds' eggs or nests (students, parents, or the science department in your middle or high school are possible sources for these). Put the displays in a case or in a safe place so curious students won't damage them.

Some suitable research questions for this theme include the following:

1. What is the state bird of Maryland?
2. What is the state bird of Louisiana?

3. How many books do we have under the subject heading "birds"?
4. What is the largest kind of bird living today?
5. What is the smallest bird?
6. What is the fastest flying bird?

Answers

1. Baltimore oriole   2. eastern brown pelican   3. varies   4. North African ostrich   5. bee hummingbird   6. large white-throated spine-tailed swift (The last three answers are from the *Guinness Book of World Records.*)

If your theme centers on books or libraries, ask questions that can be answered using author research books such as *The Junior Book of Authors.*

OTHER IDEAS: _____

_____

_____

_____

_____

_____

APRIL SKILLS CLASSES

Because National Library Week occurs in April, you may wish to have more than one skills class centered around literature appreciation. This would also be a good month to encourage students to visit the public library and get a card. Invite one of the public librarians to visit your classes and tell students about library programs, materials available for check-out, and how to get a library card. Even better, walk to the public library with your classes if you are close enough, or schedule a bus. Grade four is good for these visits since by then many students are allowed to go to the library alone.

Students in any grade enjoy working in pairs or in teams on a research scavenger hunt. Give each team a copy of the April Scavenger Hunt (version A is for grades three and four; version B is for grades five and above). Start each team on a different question so they won't all need the same reference sources at the same time. Students enjoy it when you use a stopwatch and record the time of each team. Post the winning time on a bulletin board with the names of the winners. If you save this information from year to year, students like to try to beat the previous year's time. Remind them that there is to be no running and that all answers are to be spelled correctly, since they have a reference source to refer to. The time for each team is not established until all their answers are correct.

APRIL RESEARCH SCAVENGER HUNT (A)

1. Who is the author of *Rabbit Hill?* _____

2. Look up *Easter* in the encyclopedia. On which page does it begin? _____

3. Look up the word *Passover* in the dictionary. What is it? _____

4. Look up *holiday* in the encyclopedia. Name one subheading. _____

5. Does our library have subject cards for *Easter?* _____
   If so, what is the title of one book about Easter? _____

6. Look up *rabbit* in the encyclopedia. Name one subheading. _____

7. Look up *rabbit* in the dictionary. What are the guide words on the page where you found the word? _____ and _____

8. April 1 is April Fool's Day. Is there a subject card in the card catalog for *April Fool's Day?*
   _____

9. On April Fool's Day people play jokes. Look in the card catalog under the heading "Jokes and Riddles" and write the title of one book with that subject heading.
   _____

10. Look up *April* in the encyclopedia. Give one fact about April that you did not know before.
    _____
    _____

APRIL RESEARCH SCAVENGER HUNT (B)

1. Make a call slip for a nonfiction book about rabbits.
   Write it here:

   _____

   _____

   _____

2. On what day of the week will April Fool's Day fall in the

   year 2015? _____

3. List one audiovisual item the library has about Easter.

   _____

4. Look up *Passover* in the encyclopedia. What is it? _____

5. Using the almanac, find the subject *Eggs*. List two of the subheadings given.

   _____

   _____

6. Use an encyclopedia and look up *April Fool's Day*. Give one fact that you did not know

   before. _____

   _____

7. Using a geographical dictionary, find the subject *Easter Island*. Give one fact about

   Easter Island. _____

   _____

8. Who said, "April, April, Laugh thy girlish laughter; Then, the moment after, Weep thy

   girlish tears"? _____

9. In some places there is a lot of rain in April. Using a thesaurus, find two other words to

   use in place of the word *rain*. _____ and _____

10. Find a magazine article about the earth (since Earth Day is in April). Give the title of the

    article, the magazine it is in, and the month and year of the magazine. _____

    _____

    _____

Let third graders and able second graders find books in the easy and fiction section using call numbers written on the bunny cards provided here. Write in appropriate call numbers and titles, and then laminate the cards.

Answers to the Scavenger Hunts are as follows:

April Scavenger Hunt A Answers

1. Robert Lawson
2. varies
3. a Jewish religious holiday in memory of the freeing of the Jews from Egypt

4–10. answers vary

April Scavenger Hunt B Answers

1. varies
2. Wednesday
3. varies
4. a Jewish holiday commemorating the freeing of the Jews from captivity in Egypt
5. consumption per capita

    export & import

    nutritive value

    prices-farm

    production by state
6. varies
7. varies but could be such things as 46 sq. miles, highest point 1765 feet, has gigantic statues, discovered on Easter Sunday 1722 by a Dutch admiral and his crew.
8. Sir William Watson
9. Some answers could be: precipitation, drencher, downpour, torrent, shower, sprinkle etc.
10. varies

Another seasonal way to give students extra practice in locating books is to put the call numbers in brightly colored plastic eggs, which can be purchased at most stores selling Easter items. Put the eggs in a large basket and let each student draw one egg. Each egg should contain a different call slip for a book about spring or Easter. If you have many books on these subjects, you can use many eggs, divide the class into teams, give each team a basket, and see which team can fill its basket first by finding items in an egg. The item must be found before an egg can be placed in the team basket.

CALL NUMBER SLIPS

If you have had third graders make their own books, as suggested in March, review what they learned about books by asking them a question about a book they plan to check out. For instance, "What is the copyright date of your book?" "Where was your book published?" "Who is the publisher?" Ask only one question each week, and change the question each week so students will become thoroughly familiar with the information found in a book.

OTHER IDEAS: _____

_____

_____

_____

APRIL STORYTIMES

Because of National Library Week, this is a good month to emphasize some of the excellent Caldecott Medal winners and Caldecott Honor books. Explain to the students that the medal is given for the best picture book of the year, and talk to them about illustrations. Even young children can learn to recognize an author's style. If you read several William Steig books, for example, and then in another session show students another Steig book and ask them who illustrated it, many will know. Other easily identified illustrators are Tomie DePaola, Marc Brown, and Harry Allard.

The Talking Eggs, by Robert San Souci. This 1990 Honor book is one of the best. It is not only beautifully illustrated, but it is fun to read and holds children spellbound. It is a modern fairy tale best suited to students in at least grade two. It follows the formula of a younger sister being kinder than her older sister and thus winning riches, but it is different enough to captivate the students.

King Bidgood's in the Bathtub, by Audrey Wood, illustrated by Don Wood. This is a 1986 Honor book. Both the illustrations and the story are entertaining. Children will laugh as King Bidgood refuses to leave his bathtub for any reason!

The Garden of Abduhl Gazazi, by Chris Van Allsburg. This 1980 Honor book is beautifully illustrated in black and white pencil drawings, and the story is equally good. A boy is taking care of neighbor's bad-tempered dog. He takes the dog for a walk and it runs onto land owned by an imposing magician. The magician, Abduhl Gazazi, convinces the boy that the dog has been turned into a duck, which flies off with the boy's hat in its bill. The ending is satisfying, because the literal minded will have an explanation for the return of the dog and the hat, while the more magically inclined will have a magical explanation. Second-grade students especially enjoy this book.

The Judge, by Harve Zemach, illustrated by Margot Zemach. This is a 1970 Honor book that is still fun to read, especially to first graders. Prisoners describe a "horrible monster" which is coming. Each prisoner tells something more, but the judge does not believe any of them. On the last page, the monster is revealed, much to the children's delight. If you have time during storytime, let the students have paper and crayons and draw the monster before you reveal the final page.

The following books are not Caldecott winners, but they do please children and should be readily available.

Josephina Hates Her Name, by Diana Engel. Josephina hates her name and all her friends make fun of it until one day Grandma tells her about her Great Aunt Josephina, whom she is named for. This book could easily lead into discussions about self-esteem, so it might be a good one to recommend to teachers for use in the classroom. Best for grades two and three.

Books Are for Eating, by Sherry Walton. Katy tries to prove that she could never have been as silly as her little brother Alex, as she contrasts what she *knows* and what little Alex *thinks.* For example, she knows books are to be read, but Alex thinks they are to be eaten. In the end, Katy finds one thing that she and Alex can agree on. For kindergarten and grade one.

Max's Chocolate Chicken, by Rosemary Wells. Max finds a chocolate chicken, but his sister Ruby says that the one who finds the most eggs gets to eat the chicken. Max is good at finding mud puddles and acorns, but not at finding eggs. The result is unpredictable! For kindergarten.

OTHER TITLES YOU LIKE: _____

_____

_____

_____

_____

_____

_____

_____ *APRIL BOOK TALKS* _____

When planning book talks for older students, don't forget to show them picture books that may intrigue them, both for the beautiful illustrations and for the ideas or humor that they may have missed when they were younger. A great example of one of these is *The Mysteries of Harris Burdick,* by Chris Van Allsburg. Show students this book and read them the introductions, and they will be excited about reading the opening sentences that accompany each exciting and sometimes baffling illustration. Many will wish to finish one or more of the stories with their own creative writing. This is a great book to recommend to teachers as a stimulus to writing lessons.

Other Caldecott winners that are great to read or show to older students include *The Polar Express, The Wreck of the Zephyr,* both also by Chris Van Allsburg, *Fables,* by Arnold Lobel, *Castle,* by David Macaulay, and *Duffy and the Devil,* by Harve Zemach.

Newbery winners are often difficult for students in grades four, five, and six to read on their own, but they are received well when the teacher reads them to the class. Books of this type to recommend for classroom reading include *My Brother Sam is Dead,* by James and Christopher Collier (good to recommend to teachers who are discussing the American Revolution), *Roll of Thunder, Hear My Cry,* by Mildred Taylor, *Julie of the Wolves,* by Jean Craighead George, and *The Hero and the Crown,* by Robin McKinley.

Some Newbery winners students can enjoy independently are good to feature in your book talks this month: *Bridge to Terabithia,* by Katherine Paterson, *Ramona and her Father, Dear Mr. Henshaw,* and *Ramona Quimby, Age 8,* all by Beverly Cleary, and *Mrs. Frisby and the Rats of NIMH,* by Robert O'Brien. The 1989 winner, *Joyful Noise: Poems for Two Voices,* by Paul Fleischman, is one students will enjoy, especially if you copy one of the poems and let the students take parts.

OTHER TITLES YOU LIKE: _____

_____

_____

_____

_____

_____

_____

LMC MANAGEMENT

Donated Books and Magazines

People often wish to donate books or magazines to the library. These can be a helpful addition, or a nuisance (if, for example, you are inundated with numerous back issues of *National Geographic*). If the donation is of a magazine you already have in abundance, it is still best to accept the gift gracefully. Ask the person donating the magazines if it is all right with them if students cut them up. If there is no objection, let teachers use these for students to cut up for reports or creative writing. Teachers will often come to you for magazines to cut up, and donated copies of *Ranger Rick, National Geographic, Your Big Backyard,* and so on are good for this purpose.

At other times, people might wish to donate a book to your library in memory of someone. Sometimes they will bring you a new book, but often they will ask you to buy the book and then they will pay for it, since they feel you have more knowledge of what your library needs. When buying a book in memory of someone, try to buy a beautiful book that will last a long time and not be dated soon. For example, Tomie DePaola's beautiful book of poetry would be a better selection than a book from some popular series such as The Babysitter's Club or Choose Your Own Adventure Books. These books are popular and should by all means be purchased, but not for a book given in memory.

When the book arrives, place a bookplate in it that says, "In memory of _____." Let the person donating the book be the first to check it out. It is a good idea to make a list of books donated to the library, including the name of the donor, the title of the books, and the reason for the donation. Sometimes people come back in a few months or years and ask to see the book they donated, and it is embarrassing if you forget which was theirs. A form for recording this information is provided.

April is a good time to talk to the parent organization in your school to see if they would be interested in starting a custom that students who wish to do so may donate a book to the library on their birthday. The donated book should have an appropriate bookplate: "This book was donated by _____ in honor of his/her _____ birthday."

MEMORIAL BOOK DONATIONS

DONOR	TITLE OF BOOK	REASON FOR DONATION

May

Put away your snowsuits,
Your sleds, your warm wool hats!
Get out your bikes and
    jump-ropes,
Your baseballs and your bats!
Pack away your sweaters,
Your coats, and skiing gear!
Unpack your shorts and
    swimsuits,
It's warm when May is here!

May Calendar

The end of the school year draws nearer, but there is still time to teach that special skill or have a great reading incentive activity. Plan exciting events for this last full month.

May 1	May Day
May 5	Cinco de Mayo—Mexican holiday
May 5	Children's Day in Japan
May 7, 1833	Birthdate of composer Johannes Brahms
May 7, 1840	Birthdate of composer Peter Tchaikovsky
May 8, 1884	Birthdate of President Harry S Truman
May 11, 1858	Minnesota entered the Union
May 12, 1820	Birthdate of Florence Nightingale
May 13, 1607	Founding of the Jamestown colony
May 18, 1980	Mt. St. Helens exploded
May 19, 1884	Ringling Brothers' first circus formed
May 20, 1884	Birthdate of French painter Henri Rousseau
May 21, 1881	American Red Cross founded by Clara Barton
May 22, 1844	Birthdate of American artist Mary Cassatt
May 23, 1788	South Carolina entered the Union
May 26, 1951	Birthdate of astronaut Sally Ride
May 29, 1917	Birthdate of President John F. Kennedy
May 29, 1790	Rhode Island entered the Union
May 29, 1848	Wisconsin entered the Union
May 31, 1819	Birthdate of American poet Walt Whitman

Check your calendar for the exact dates of

Mother's Day—second Sunday in May
Memorial Day—last Monday in May
National Music Week

———————— *MAY THEMES* ————————

A possible theme for May is, *Things Are Jumping in the Media Center.* Use frogs for research center questions, the authors corner, and so on. *Learn Something New at the Library* would fit in well if you plan to feature arts and crafts or any other how-to books this month. *Books—a Passport to Anywhere* makes a good theme. For this, feature exhibits from other countries and display both fiction and nonfiction books about various countries around the world.

OTHER IDEAS: _____

_____

_____

_____

———————— *SPECIAL DAYS IN MAY* ————————

May 5 is Children's Day in Japan. Feature books about this country, and try to find a speaker from Japan or of Japanese descent to talk to classes about this holiday. Display Japanese toys or kites, which you can find in import markets.

May 5 is also the Cinco de Mayo celebration in Mexico. Invite a speaker from Mexico or of Mexican descent to speak to classes about the celebration. Display books about Mexico or the holiday. Make a large Mexican flag for a bulletin board, and display pictures of Mexico and the Cinco de Mayo celebration.

OTHER IDEAS: _____

_____

_____

_____

_____

———————— *MAY BULLETIN BOARDS* ————————

Some schools end the school year in May. If your school closes this month, you may wish to use one of the bulletin boards in the June chapter.

Ideas for May include "Jump for a Good Book," a bulletin board that features a frog and fits in well with the theme, *Things Are Jumping in the Media Center.* For this bulletin board, use a blue background. Use the pattern at the end of the chapter to make a large leaping frog and the lily pad patterns to make lily pads on which you can write book titles or staple book jackets.

"Learn Something New from Books" is a simple bulletin board to make and gives you an opportunity to advertise the many books that can show children how to do something. Possible candidates include arts and crafts books, science experiment books, calligraphy books, cookbooks, foreign language books, and so on. If you plan to have a bulletin board in the arts and crafts corner advertising those books, don't feature them on this bulletin board. Encourage students to check out books that teach them something and bring to the library anything they have learned to make. Display these items on a table or shelf, keeping them safe from curious hands by covering them with plastic wrap or placing them high out of reach. Students who learn poetry or a few lines of a foreign language can demonstrate what they've learned.

MAY AUTHORS BIRTHDAY CLUB

Choose several or all of the many good authors born in May to feature on your authors bulletin board. Talk to students in your various classes about the featured authors, and display their books. A pattern for the frogs to arrange around the birthday cake is provided at the end of this chapter.

Since for many schools the school year is coming to an end, this may be the last month for an authors birthday club party. Make it a special one. If the weather is nice, you might have the party outside under a tree and invite a storyteller to come and tell the students stories. Ice cream bars and popsicles served outdoors are always a treat. You might want to recognize students who have participated in three or four previous authors' parties and encourage students to read during the summer. If you plan to do the summer authors birthday party (see June), introduce it to the students and encourage them to participate in it. Have a drawing for prizes and small gifts for each participant.

OTHER IDEAS: _____

_____

_____

_____

MAY CONTEST CORNER

Here's a contest that children enjoy and that makes them use their creative thinking skills: Post several pictures of animals doing things, labeling each with a number. Pictures of chimps and monkeys are especially good for this, but puppies and kittens also make good subjects. Provide answer sheets numbered with as many numbers as there are posted pictures, and ask students to write what they

May Authors

LOVE THOSE AUTHORS!

May 3, 1947	Mavis Jukes
May 4, 1932	Beverly Butler
May 4, 1945	Don Wood
May 5, 1910	Leo Lionni
May 6, 1931	Judy Delton
May 6, 1937	Susan Ferris
May 6, 1942	Guilio Maestro
May 7, 1932	Nonny Hogrogian
May 9, 1860	Sir James Barrie
May 9, 1916	William Pene DuBois
May 9, 1916	Eleanor Estes
May 9, 1914	Keith Robertson
May 11, 1927	Zilpha Keatley Snyder
May 12, 1812	Edward Lear
May 12, 1921	Farley Mowat
May 13, 1938	Francine Pascal
May 16, 1928	Betty Miles
May 18, 1925	Lillian Hoban
May 18, 1907	Irene Hunt
May 20, 1917	Don Lawson
May 22, 1933	Arnold Lobel
May 23, 1902	Scott O'Dell
May 25, 1943	Barbara Bottner
May 26, 1934	Sheila Greenwald
May 29, 1938	Brock Cole
May 30, 1912	Millicent Selsam
May 31, 1914	Jay Williams
May 31, 1935	Henry Mazer

think each animal is saying. A caption of "What Are They Saying?" and a background border for each picture are all you need for a colorful bulletin board contest. Post some of the best answers under the appropriate pictures. You and the students can choose the best for each picture, or you can make it a noncompetitive contest and post all the entries.

A "Guess How Many Books Are in Our Library?" contest would be appropriate for the end of the year. Award a small prize to the student whose guess is closest. Students will be amazed at the number of books there are.

The riddle spot could feature frog or bug riddles this month if you used the frog patterns for your research and author corners. Write each buggy riddle on one of the cards held by a frog. Many frog riddles can be found in various joke books, but if you can't find enough they are easily adapted from jokes featuring other animals. (For example, "Why did the frog cross the road? To get to the other side.") Most ordinary riddles adapt well.

If appropriate for your part of the country, you could also read some frog stories and tell or read Mark Twain's "The Jumping Frog of Calaveras County," and then hold a frog-jumping contest.

OTHER IDEAS: _____

_____

_____

_____

_____ MAY ARTS AND CRAFTS _____
CORNER

Two famous artists who can be featured this month are Henri Rousseau, born May 20, 1844, and Mary Cassatt, born May 22, 1844. Display prints of their work and a brief biography of each. One section of the art corner could be reserved for a bulletin board display of arts and crafts books. Use a caption like "Hands On Fun!" or "Make It Yourself!" and accompany each book jacket with a construction paper hand in a bright color. (The pattern is included at the end of this chapter.) Ask students to bring in art or craft items they have made following directions in a book. Display these along with the book or a copy of the page from the book so students can try to do the craft themselves. Books on paper crafts, weaving, calligraphy, and so on are all appropriate and often have directions students can follow.

OTHER IDEAS: _____

_____

_____

_____

MAY NONFICTION CORNER

Feature books about summer sports like swimming, backpacking, boating, skateboarding, baseball, and so on. You may also want to feature books about vacation places, such as national parks, theme parks, and so on.

You can use the frog patterns from the authors corner bulletin board for your research questions this month. Questions appropriate for May include the following:

1. Our thirty-third president was born on May 8, 1884. Who was he?

2. A famous author, born May 25, 1803, wrote "Nothing great was ever achieved without enthusiasm." Who was he?

3. On May 18, 1882, Massachusetts became the first state to pass a law stating that children must go to school. How many school districts are there in your state?

4. John F. Kennedy, thirty-fifth president of the United States, was born May 29, 1917. He was the youngest man ever elected to that office. How old was he when he took office?

5. Memorial Day is celebrated the last Monday in May. In what year was the first Memorial Day celebrated?

Answers

1. Harry S Truman   2. Ralph Waldo Emerson   3. varies   4. 43   5. May 5, 1866, at Waterloo, New York

If there have been some students who usually answer the research questions of the month, honor them in your skills classes and award them a small prize. You might wish to award them a certificate naming them research experts.

OTHER IDEAS: _____

_____

_____

_____

MAY SKILLS CLASSES

By this time of year, you have probably introduced all the skills you plan to teach in each grade, so May is a good time to review the various skills. The best way to review the skills is with a team activity the children enjoy.

A team activity similar to the one detailed in February is appropriate now to help grades four and five review the use of the almanac, encyclopedia, card catalog, *Guinness Book of World Records,* and dictionary. Divide the class into four teams.

REFERENCE REVIEW CONTEST CARDS

Team 1. BASKETBALL

1. Who invented the game of basketball?
2. What is the address of the Los Angeles Lakers?
3. Which NBA team has won the most championships?
4. What is the title and call number of a book in this library about basketball?
5. What is the definition for *basketball?*

Team 2. FOOTBALL

1. When was the game of football first played?
2. What is the address of the Los Angeles Rams?
3. What was the shortest touchdown pass?
4. What is the definition of the word *punt?*
5. What is the title and call number of a book in this library about football?

Team 3. SOCCER

1. What is the title and call number of a book in this library about soccer?
2. What was the longest soccer match?
3. When was soccer first played?
4. What is the definition of *soccer?*
5. Who won the World Cup for Soccer in 1982?

Team 4. BASEBALL

1. Who was the shortest major league baseball player?
2. Who won the World Series in 1981?
3. What is the definition of the word *bunt?*
4. What is the title and call number of a book in this library about baseball?
5. Baseball developed from what early English sport?

Each team sits together at a table with the appropriate reference materials and a card with five questions to be answered from the materials and the card catalog. Provide each team with a pencil and paper for answers, or transfer the questions from the cards to a worksheet. The cards are easier, however, since each table has a different set of questions and they can be reused.

Each card could be of a different color. On the back of each, write the reference books you want students to use. Students begin when you say "start!"; you can time the activity if you wish. It's up to the students to choose among their reference sources for information. When they have answered all their questions, they raise their hands and you check their answers and record their time. They are not finished until all their answers are correct. Most teams seem to be able to complete this activity in twenty minutes or less.

Answer Key

Team 1: Basketball Use these references: a *B* volume of an encyclopedia, an almanac, a *Guinness Book of World Records,* and a dictionary. 1. James Naismith (encyclopedia) 2. Los Angeles Lakers, P.O. Box 10, Inglewood, CA 90306 (1989 *World Almanac*) 3. Boston Celtics, with sixteen as of 1990 (1990 *Guinness Book of World Records*) 4. varies according to your collection 5. varies by dictionary

Team 2: Football Use these references: an *F* volume of an encyclopedia, an almanac, a *Guinness Book of World Records,* and a dictionary. 1. early 1800s (encyclopedia) 2. Los Angeles Rams, 2327 West Lincoln Ave., Anaheim, CA 92801 (almanac) 3. two inches—Dallas Cowboys on October 9, 1960 (1990 *Guinness*) 4. varies by dictionary 5. varies by collection

Team 3: Soccer Use these references: an *S* volume of an encyclopedia, an almanac, a *Guinness Book of World Records,* and a dictionary. 1. varies by collection 2. seventy-five-and-a-half hours by two teams trying to set a record (1990 *Guinness*—earlier editions list a shorter time from an actual game) 3. A game like soccer was played as early as 400 B.C. (*World Book Encyclopedia*) 4. varies by dictionary 5. Italy (almanac)

Team 4: Baseball Use these references: a *B* volume of an encyclopedia, an almanac, a dictionary, and a *Guinness Book of World Records.* 1. Eddie Gaebel, a three-foot, seven-inch pinch hitter for the St. Louis Browns (*Guinness*) 2. Los Angeles—National League (almanac) 3. varies by dictionary 4. varies by collection 5. rounders (*World Book Encyclopedia*)

————— *MAY SPECIAL: THE READ-AWAY* ————— *AIRLINES READING PROGRAM*

If your school is not dismissed until later in June and you prefer to wait until then for the summer reading program, you still have time for one last reading activity in May. With vacation time so near, it is a perfect time to encourage students to embark on the Read-Away Airlines for a wonderful trip via books. Since this reading program is based on minutes read rather than the number of books read, it is good for students of all reading abilities.

While students need not read books about other countries, you may want to introduce the program by showing them fiction and nonfiction books about far-away places.

Students decide how much they want to read. Each destination takes two hours. A student picks a place to visit and writes it on a Read-Away Airlines ticket (the form is provided). After reading for two hours, he or she has a parent sign the ticket and returns it to you. You tear off the ticket and give the student an "I Flew to _____" endorsement. The endorsement is stapled or glued to the inside of the passport. The torn-off ticket is then deposited in a box for a prize drawing at the end of the program. Give each student a colored flag on which to write his or her name. He or she then pins it to the appropriate destination on a large map of the world posted somewhere in the library. Another destination can be chosen if desired, using the same procedure.

As an added activity, students can do a postcard book report. On the printed side of the card, they write their name and address. Then they write a letter to themselves from one of the characters in the book they just read. The character could describe where he or she lives (the setting). On the blank side of the postcard, students draw a picture of someplace described in the book. These make a nice display in the library (forms are provided).

At the end of the Read-Away Airlines Reading Program, have a party or an assembly to honor those who participated. Draw prizes using the tickets in the box. Ask students to bring their passports to show others how many places they have "flown" to. You can also award small prizes for each destination.

Preparing the Materials

Print enough passports for each participant. The passports look best on card-stock weight paper in blue. Cut the two apart and fold on the dotted line. Instruct students to write their name somewhere on their passports. "I Flew to _____" endorsements will be stapled or glued inside this passport.

Before photocopying the ticket folders, write your name under "authorized travel agent." Try to use heavier stock than bond for the folders in some attractive color. You need one for each participant. Fold in thirds along the dotted lines. The tickets will be stapled to the inside middle portion of the folder, then torn out and replaced as each destination is reached and a new one chosen.

The "I Flew to _____" endorsements and tickets can be printed on any color bond-weight paper. Print enough so some participants can have several of each. Postcards should be printed on heavier paper and should be white or a light color, since the students will be drawing on them.

PASSPORT

OFFICIAL
DOCUMENT

*United Libraries
of America*

PASSPORT

OFFICIAL
DOCUMENT

*United Libraries
of America*

TICKET

READ-AWAY
Airlines

AUTHORIZED TRAVEL AGENT:

FLIGHT			
TO			
SEAT			
GATE			

Endorsements

I FLEW TO: _____	I FLEW TO: _____	I FLEW TO: _____
I FLEW TO: _____	I FLEW TO: _____	I FLEW TO: _____
I FLEW TO: _____	I FLEW TO: _____	I FLEW TO: _____
I FLEW TO: _____	I FLEW TO: _____	I FLEW TO: _____
I FLEW TO: _____	I FLEW TO: _____	I FLEW TO: _____

TICKET

READ-AWAY
Airlines

Date: _____

Passenger: _____

Minutes: | 15 | 15 | 15 | 15 | 15 | 15 | 15 | 15 |

Time:

Destination: _____

Flight: _____ Signature _____

TICKET

READ-AWAY
Airlines

Date: _____

Passenger: _____

Minutes: | 15 | 15 | 15 | 15 | 15 | 15 | 15 | 15 |

Time:

Destination: _____

Flight: _____ Signature _____

TICKET

READ-AWAY
Airlines

Date: _____

Passenger: _____

Minutes: | 15 | 15 | 15 | 15 | 15 | 15 | 15 | 15 |

Time:

Destination: _____

Flight: _____ Signature _____

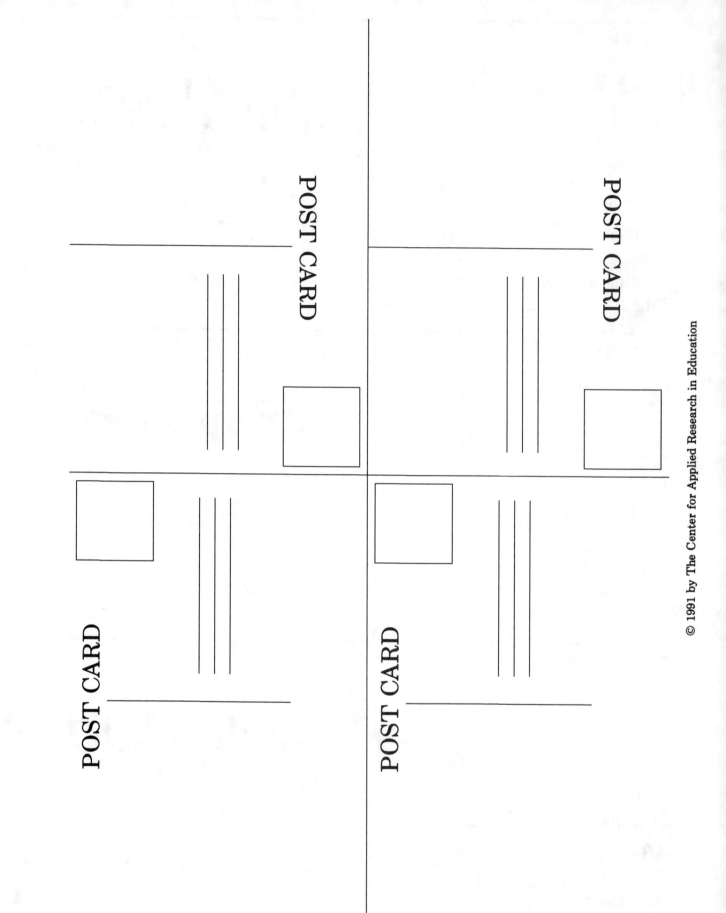

_____ *MAY STORYTIMES* _____

If your library will be closing during this month, use the storytime sessions to promote the summer authors birthday club. Explain how it works (see June) and review some of the books.

The Doorbell Rang, by Pat Hutchins. This is fun for students in kindergarten. In this story, Mom has made a platter of cookies and the children are going to divide them. They look delicious, but Mom says, "No one makes cookies like Grandma." The doorbell rings and rings, each time bringing more friends to share the cookies. At last there is only one cookie for each child, and then the doorbell rings again! Luckily it is someone who saves the day.

Company's Coming, by Arthur Yorinks, illustrated by David Small. Shirley and Moe are expecting company when a flying saucer quietly lands in the yard. The spacemen who emerge from it speak English and are surprisingly polite. Shirley invites them for dinner and they leave, saying they will return at six o'clock. Moe is scared and calls the FBI, which calls the Pentagon, which calls the Army, Navy, and Air Force. When the spacemen return, bearing a suspicious-looking gift, the house is surrounded by all of the armed forces. The gift is a surprise to all. This is best for grades one and two.

The Three Sillies, retold and illustrated by Paul Galdone. This one makes second and third graders laugh and gasp at the silly things the characters do. It is a story of a girl and her family who do such silly things that her boyfriend refuses to marry her until he can find three people sillier than they are. The story will be new to most of the students, and they enjoy it.

Jimmy's Boa and the Big Splash Birthday Bash, by Trinka Hakes Noble. Jimmy's mother thinks a goldfish will be a harmless gift for his birthday party, but when he takes both the new goldfish and his pet boa to his birthday party at the aquarium, bedlam results. This third book about Jimmy and his boa is as much fun as the earlier two.

The Mother's Day Sandwich, by Jillian Wynot. Ivy and her little brother want to surprise their mother by making her breakfast in bed. It turns out to be more of a surprise than they intended. For kindergarten through second grade.

There are so many good authors in the summer group that you can choose your favorites from Frank Asch, Verna Aardema, Eric Carle, Peggy Parish, Maurice Sendak, Chris Van Allsburg, and others. Don't forget to show the students some books by Matt Christopher, since his books are good for students just beginning to read books other than picture books. Have an array of books displayed at each class.

OTHER TITLES YOU LIKE: _____

_____

_____

_____

_____

———————————— *MAY BOOK TALKS* ————————————

If May is the last month you will have library classes, check the June section on the summer reading club for ideas about introducing it to students. If you will have classes, just mention the club briefly to students and explain that the books you are reviewing are by authors born during the summer months. The following three are by summer authors:

The Burning Questions of Bingo Brown, by Betsy Byars. In this entertaining and amusing book, Bingo Brown, now in the sixth grade, has begun to wonder about life and girls. In his class journal he writes what he calls "burning questions," such as, "Has a principal ever expelled an entire school?" and "Why do people care if I see their papers?" Between worries about his teacher and a planned school protest about wearing T shirts with words on them, Bingo also has time to get interested in Melissa. Display many of Betsy Byars's books—the children will like them. There are several audiovisual kits and videos about her books that could also be shown.

Double Dog Dare, by Jamie Gilson. This is another of Gilson's stories about Hobie Hanson, and just as amusing. Hobie, now in fifth grade, feels that perhaps he isn't as smart as Nick, his best friend, or Molly, because they are going to be in the gifted and talented program this year. However, Hobie has found out about some mints that, when crunched in the dark, make sparks fly. He also knows that sugar-free mints will not do this. He gets Molly to try this with him, telling her that the smarter you are the more sparks will fly when the mint is crunched. As you can imagine, he gives Molly a sugar-free mint, while his contains sugar. He also gets out of a double-dare to kiss Molly with an agility that shows he may not be in the gifted and talented program, but he has a quick mind and a sense of humor.

Jamie Gilson has written many books. Display several. Boys especially enjoy them.

Christina's Ghost, by Betty Ren Wright. This is another book by the popular author of *The Dollhouse Murders.* Christina helps to solve a mystery of a young boy who appears and disappears, never speaking; and with her Uncle Ralph she gets rid of an ominous, ghostly being. Betty Ren Wright's books are enticing and readable. Most children enjoy them, so have a good supply of this and her other books to show the children.

OTHER TITLES YOU LIKE: _____

_____

_____

_____

_____

_____

_____

_____ *LMC MANAGEMENT* _____

Computerizing

There will come a time, if it hasn't come already, when you will have to decide whether to computerize your library. Undoubtedly, prices will come down on computer systems, but for now, with prices high, you need to consider whether the benefit to your library will be worth the expense. If your library is small, it probably is not, but if it is large—and your budget for aides has not increased with the size of the collection—it may be worthwhile.

Computer systems are expensive and time-consuming to install. Their benefit lies in a better control of books, software, and equipment, faster inventory, and faster check-out. They are useful for making overdue lists and for keeping track of books a student has borrowed, especially when that student is moving from your district. Computers can quickly generate subject bibliographies for a student or teacher.

If you decide that you do need a computer, you will have to consult the administration, since you will not want the entire expense to be taken from your book, equipment, or software budget. Once the decision is made that computerizing is feasible, start planning immediately.

First, get information on several different systems. If schools near you have systems, try to visit them and talk to the librarians about the advantages and disadvantages of their system. The librarians will be able to help you plan when and how the system can be installed. Some systems are integrated and link the card catalog with the check-out and inventory program. In others you can later add a card catalog program. If the price difference is not too great, the integrated system is better, since you will have to close the library only once for installation. Check as thoroughly as you can into the advantages and disadvantages of each system, because it is a big expense and almost impossible to redo if the system you choose is either inadequate or impractical for your situation.

Once you have selected a company's system, plan with the representative of that company how best to install it. Try to get your principal or supervisor to plan with you, since he or she needs to understand how much time is involved as well as the advantages of the system. Many school districts begin installation in the last two or three weeks of the school year, so the library is closed to teachers and students only a little longer than usual. Because of the closing, however, teachers also must be informed about the benefits of the system.

Most, if not all, of the companies that supply these systems have someone who will train you both in how to get your collection on the computer and how to run it. They can usually train you and one other person, probably your aide if you have one. Then you can train volunteers to help you get the collection on computer and bar code the books. If possible, try to have the entire book collection on the computer before checking out to students.

In addition to the two weeks at the end of the year, plan to devote time during the summer to getting your collection on line. Use volunteers, if possible. If this is not possible because of financial considerations, try to have the library closed at the beginning of the school year until at least the book portion of your collection is on line. Librarians who have tried to conduct classes, check out books, and computerize the collection at the same time have said that this is difficult and impractical.

As the prices of computer systems come down, you can expect most libraries to become computerized. Careful planning can ensure that you choose the best system for your situation and install it in the least disruptive way.

PATTERNS

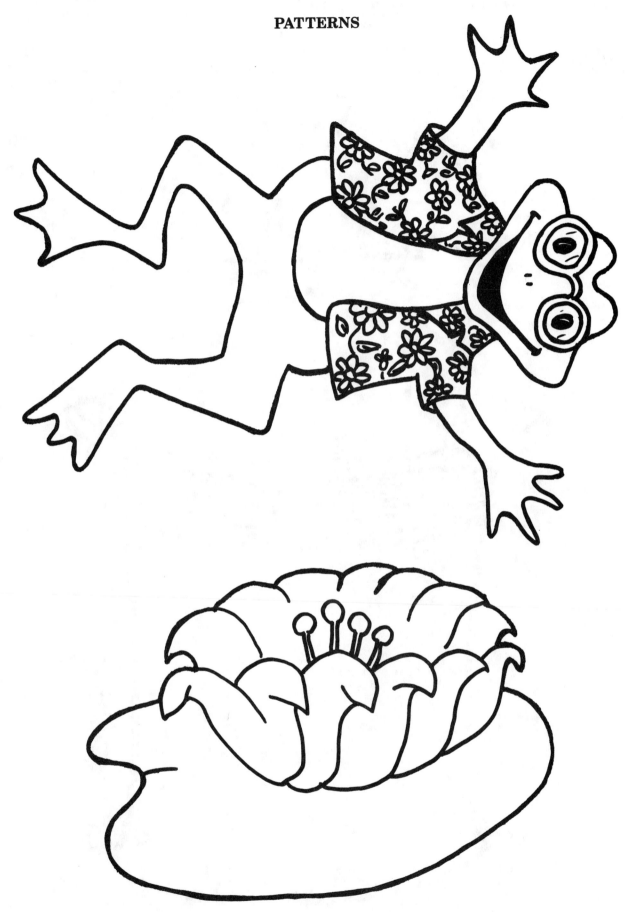

June

Sunny sands, blue sky,
A lazy day and kites to fly!
A picnic in a shady park,
Then fireworks sparkling after dark.
Enjoy each golden, sun-drenched day,
For summer's here, it's time to play!

June Calendar

At last—the end to a great year! Prepare for a good beginning next year by planning a successful closing this year.

June 1, 1792	Kentucky entered the Union
June 1, 1796	Tennessee entered the Union
June 7	Freedom of the Press Day
June 7, 1848	Birthdate of French artist Paul Gauguin
June 7, 1917	Birthdate of Gwendolyn Brooks, first African American to win a Pulitzer Prize
June 9, 1934	Donald Duck first appeared
June 12, 1839	According to legend, date of the first baseball game, in Cooperstown, New York
June 12, 1924	Birthdate of President George Bush
June 14	Flag Day—the original U.S. flag was adopted on this day in 1777
June 15, 1836	Arkansas entered the Union
June 20, 1868	West Virginia entered the Union
June 21, 1788	New Hampshire entered the Union and thereby put the Constitution into effect
June 25, 1788	Virginia entered the Union
June 27, 1880	Birthdate of Helen Keller

Check your calendar for the exact dates of

Father's Day (third Sunday in June)
First day of summer (on or near June 21)

JUNE: A HAPPY ENDING
TO A SUCCESSFUL YEAR

Most school libraries will be closing this month. To get all materials turned in before the students leave for the summer, it is necessary to end your regular library schedule a week or two before the last day of school. Since most school librarians teach from 60 to 90 percent of the time, there is not enough time during the year to keep up with such important tasks as weeding and evaluating the collection, taking inventory, checking audiovisual equipment, and studying reviews and catalogs to make orders for the coming year.

While teachers prefer you to hold classes as long as possible, most are understanding once you explain to them about your need to get materials checked in, stored, and inventoried. Use faculty meetings or written messages to let them know that getting these things done helps you to know your collection, keep it in good condition, and obtain the materials they need for teaching.

The length of time you will need depends on how large your collection is and also whether you have an extended contract that allows you a few days to a week after the school year ends. If you have an extended contract, you still need some time to get materials back before students depart, but you can leave the inventory, ordering, and so on until school closes. Meet with your administrator to determine the best time for your regular schedule to end. Make sure that he or she understands the importance of getting materials in before the students leave and why weeding and inventory are important. Try to determine the date as early as possible so you can make your plans for the month of June.

IF YOU HAVE CLASSES
THIS MONTH

June Themes

Possible themes for this month include *Read for a Great Summer, Vacation with Books,* or *On a Hot Day, Read a Book.* Other ideas to encourage summer reading can be found in the summer authors birthday club section.

June Bulletin Boards

If you are open for classes at all in June, you will want your bulletin boards to be attractive and to encourage students to continue their reading during the summer months. "Going on Vacation? Don't Forget to Pack a Book!" can feature either summer titles or vacation spots. Use real travel stickers on the suitcase and a real (used) ticket or travel brochure in the bear's paw.

For "Swim, Picnic, and Play! But Don't Forget to Read!" you can use colorful wallpaper scraps for the swimming trunks and grass cloth wallpaper for the basket. Patterns for all are at the end of this chapter.

Corner Ideas

You probably won't have enough time with the children to run an authors birthday club for the month or a nonfiction research contest. The contest corner also will not be practical. In the arts and crafts corner, you might post the photos you have taken of all the student and teacher artists who have displayed their work this year. Set up a caption such as "Through the Year with Art," and post the month beside each picture.

In place of the usual contests, post any advertisements you might have for the public library's summer reading program, or for other events or activities taking place in your city this summer. In the nonfiction corner, post book jackets of good nonfiction books with the caption, "Read to Learn." You can use remaining skills classes to interest children in participating in a summer reading program—either one you are sponsoring or one the public library offers.

OTHER IDEAS: _____

_____

_____

_____

ENCOURAGING SUMMER READING

A Letter to Parents

Provided here is a sample letter to parents about the need to encourage their children to read. Adapt it to your particular situation. If you plan on a summer reading program, include a paragraph about it in your letter. Send the letter home with students during the last week of school.

Summer Authors Birthday Club

One way to encourage student reading during the summer is to sponsor a summer authors birthday club. Students who have enjoyed the birthday parties during the school year will probably be enthusiastic. If you want to sponsor this program, you first need to discuss it with your administrator (who will probably be enthusiastic about it) and visit the public library to make sure they are willing to make some of your program's forms available for students who either lose theirs or decide to start later in the summer. They also need to be willing to help students find appropriate books by the summer authors. Then, check with the middle or junior high school to see if fifth or sixth graders reading in the program can turn in

SUMMER'S COMING!

WHAT A GREAT TIME TO READ!

Dear Parents:

Summer is a time to relax and have fun, and it is also an excellent time for you to encourage your child to read for knowledge and for fun.

Here are some ideas that might inspire your child to discover the joys of reading!

1. Set a good example. Let your child see you relaxing with a good book or a magazine on a hot summer day.

2. Read to your child as often as you can. Even older children enjoy having a good book read to them. Pick one that you both enjoy and relax and read in a shady, pleasant spot.

3. Play games with your child. Board games, thinking games, and strategy games all help your child to become a better reader.

4. Limit both your own and your child's television time. Playing a game together or reading a good book is more fun than reruns on television!

5. When on a trip, encourage your child to read road signs, and play alphabet games with him or her.

6. Visit the public library with your child and let him or her see you picking out books you enjoy. Show interest in his or her choices. If the library is sponsoring a summer reading program for children, encourage your child to participate.

ENJOY YOUR SUMMER
AND DON'T FORGET TO READ!

Your School Librarian

DON'T FORGET TO READ!

SUMMER AUTHORS BIRTHDAY CLUB

Primary Grades
AUTHORS WITH SUMMER BIRTHDAYS

Verna Aardema	6-6-11
Sue Alexander	8-20-33
Jose Aruego	8-9-32
Frank Asch	8-6-46
Betsy Garrett Bang	7-9-12
Virginia Burton	8-30-09
Eric Carle	6-25-29
Nancy Carlstrom	8-4-48
Matt Christopher	8-16-17
Joanna Cole	8-11-44
Patricia Coombs	7-23-26
Benjamin Elkin	8-10-11
Don Freeman	8-11-08
Paul Galdone	6-2-14
John Gantos	7-2-51
Gail Gibbons	8-1-44
Mary Ann Hoberman	8-12-30
Pat Hutchins	6-18-42
Sesyle Joslin	8-30-21
Steven Kroll	8-11-41
Karla Kuskin	7-17-32
David McPhail	6-30-40
Arlene Mosel	8-21-21
Peggy Parish	7-14-27
Diane Paterson	7-23-46
Robert Quackenbush	7-23-29
Beatrice DeRegniers	8-16-14
Richard Scarry	6-5-19
Maurice Sendak	6-10-28
Peter Spier	6-6-27
Chris Van Allsburg	6-18-49
Lynd Ward	6-26-05
E. B. White	7-11-1899
Arthur Yorinks	8-21-53

Date/Title/Author:

_____

_____

_____

_____

_____

_____

_____

_____

_____

_____

_____

_____

_____

_____

_____

_____

_____

_____

_____

_____
      signature of parent

The best book I read this summer was _____

_____, by _____.

SUMMER AUTHORS BIRTHDAY CLUB

Upper Grades
AUTHORS WITH SUMMER BIRTHDAYS

Judie Angell	7-10-37
Natalie Babbitt	7-28-32
Betsy Byars	8-7-28
Betty Cavanna	6-24-09
Matt Christopher	8-16-17
Scott Corbett	7-27-13
Helen Cresswell	7-11-36
Paula Danziger	8-18-44
Ruth Gannett	8-12-44
Jean George	7-2-19
Jamie Gilson	7-4-33
Bette Greene	6-28-34
James Howe	8-2-46
Dean Hughes	8-24-43
Shirley Hughes	7-16-27
Norton Juster	6-2-29
Jean Karl	7-29-27
Sonia Levitin	8-18-34
Christine McDonnell	7-3-49
Peggy Parish	4-14-27
Jane Sarnoff	6-25-37
Seymour Simon	8-9-31
Robert Kimmel Smith	7-31-30
E. B. White	7-11-1899
Betty Ren Wright	6-15-27
Herbert Zim	7-12-09

Date/Title/Author:

_____

_____

_____

_____

_____

_____

_____

_____

_____

_____

_____

_____

_____

_____

The best book I read this summer was _____

_____, by _____.

signature of parent

their completed forms there for either a prize or a party. That school librarian is often happy to participate, since such activities help make the library a popular place for new students. Finally, you need to photocopy the forms for the program in bright colors, preferably with two different colors, one for the primary form and the other for the intermediate form. Ali that remains then is to introduce the program to your students.

If you have time, put up the summer authors birthday club bulletin board. It will interest the students in the program even before you tell them about it. Write each author's name and birthdate on the card held in the fish's mouth. Make each fish a different color. Patterns are at the end of this chapter. You can use 3×5 cards for the authors' names, if you prefer.

Introducing the Club

In the final class for each group of students, introduce the club by explaining that each student who reads ten (or whatever number you decide) books during the summer by authors whose birthdays fall in June, July, or August will be invited to a summer authors birthday party in September. Explain the form and then introduce some of the popular books by these summer authors.

Students will often be enthusiastic and will want to check out books immediately. If there is time, let them check out one book and get a head start on their summer reading, but if there is no time, tell them to take a form and write in that title and author so they can find it at the public library. Explain to the fifth- or sixth-grade students who will be leaving the school that the middle school junior high school librarian will take the forms and hold the party for them in September.

Show second and third graders both forms, so those who are reading longer books can take the form for older students. Matt Christopher, Peggy Parish, and several other authors who write easily read fiction books are on the summer list, so these students should be able to find good books at their reading level.

Since much of the class will be spent explaining the program and answering any questions, you may only have time to display the best books of many of the authors and hold up some of the favorites while telling the title and author. There probably will not be time for longer reviews.

NO MORE CLASSES —NOW WHAT?

Getting Materials In and Stored

Now that your regular schedule is finished, the first thing you must do is work to get the checked-out materials in. A week or two before all books are due, post signs around the school announcing the due date.

When you have carded and shelved all the returned material, you will probably be dismayed to find an abundance of material still checked out. As soon as possible, make a list for each classroom of books and other materials still checked out and the name of the students who checked them out. Teachers will also need a list of materials they have checked out, because they, too, often use them and set them aside and forget them. You might wish to promise a treat to each classroom returning all materials by a certain date. To hold down expenses, you might give a popsicle to each student in the classes with all their materials in by the designated due date, and a smaller treat such as a piece of candy or a bookmark to classes whose materials are turned in by a later date but still several days before the school year ends. (This might be considered a bribe, but it offers students an incentive to get their materials in.)

Your district probably has a policy for what to do about students who don't get their material in. If possible, send letters to the parents with bills for books that are not yet in. This is time-consuming, however, so try to get the materials in before typing bills. All of this will be much simpler if you already have a computer system that prints class lists, individual bills, and so on.

Few libraries will be able to get all the materials turned in, but it is important to get as much as possible, since prices constantly increase while budgets increase little or not at all.

Inventory, Evaluation, and Weeding

Preferably, you have been evaluating and weeding your collection during the year as you see worn or outdated materials. (If you don't have time to process weeded material during the school year, have a handy box where you can put books you want to weed.) It is simple to delete the book from a computer file, but it will take longer if you are not computerized. Further weeding can be done as you inventory your books. With the shelf list in hand, match books on the shelf with the cards in your shelf list. It is faster if you have another person read the cards to you while you locate the book, quickly check to make sure the right card is in it, and evaluate it for continued use or for discard. If a book is not on the shelf, stand the shelf card up in the file until you can check any material still checked out. If the book is still missing at the end of inventory, write (in pencil) on the shelf card, "Missing" and the year. If the book is still missing in the next inventory, you can probably safely pull the cards.

Most librarians with large collections do not have time to do a complete inventory. If you cannot do all sections of the library, plan a rotation of the sections you inventory—for instance, one year do the fiction and nonfiction sections, the next year do the easy section and the software, and then repeat the rotation the following year. This way every section is inventoried at least every other year.

Inventory is a time-consuming task. Volunteers can do it for you, but it's better to do it yourself because of the need for evaluation and weeding. Some administrators may feel that inventory is not really necessary, so try to explain to them that if the card catalog has cards for books that are lost, it will become ineffective at helping students and teachers find the books and materials they need.

Checking Audiovisual Equipment

Another time-consuming task is checking the audiovisual equipment back into the media center and then checking each piece of equipment to make sure it is still in working order. Since most teachers will need the equipment for the entire school year, you will have to wait until the end of the year. To speed the job, send a note to teachers requesting them to return any equipment they are no longer using and asking them to put a note on any equipment that needs repair.

Your job will be easier if you have had the space to keep the equipment in the media center when not in use. It will also be easier if your district has audiovisual technicians who clean and repair any equipment needing attention. If this is the case, you need only put all the equipment together in an easily accessible (but secure) place and label any that needs repair. If your district does not have this service, you or a volunteer will need to dust the equipment, cover it with its cover or a plastic bag, and put it in storage for the summer. Equipment needing repair should be sent out now so it will be in good condition for the fall.

Ordering Materials

It is a good idea to keep a want file through the year containing items you wish to order. Now is the time to get out this file and make your orders. You may find that some items are no longer a high priority, so discard those brochures or catalogs or put them back in the file for future orders. There may be teachers who have requested certain audiovisual materials or books. Try to order as many of the requested items as possible. Teachers often base their book requests on recommendations in a manual.

These books are often out of print—therefore, ask teachers if they are willing to take a book of similar content if the book they requested is out of print.

Placing a large order now will ensure that necessary materials will be in the library next fall. However, don't spend all of your budget for the next year, since you are sure to have unforeseen needs. If your district sends in the purchase orders, turn your orders in to them, clearly marked "for July billing" or for whenever your fiscal year begins. If you order yourself, mark your order in the same way so you will not be billed from this year's depleted budget.

Thanking Volunteers and Aides

Don't forget to thank your volunteers and student aides. For adult volunteers, a personal note and perhaps a small, colorful bedding plant would be nice. Many schools have teas for all of the school volunteers, but since your volunteers make so many of your programs possible, something from you is a good idea.

The student aides have also been helpful—running errands, shelving, writing overdue notes, and so on. Show them you appreciate their help by throwing a small party for them. Serve popsicles or ice cream if the weather is hot, or cookies and a soft drink if it is cooler. If you have time, show an entertaining video. Award student aides a library aide certificate (see September) at the party or at the awards assembly for the entire school.

If you have a paid aide, you might want to take him or her out to lunch before the year is over. Even though he or she is paid, this aide has probably put in extra time to help you make your library program effective.

OTHER IDEAS FOR END-OF-YEAR CLOSING: _____

_____

_____

_____

Appendix

- Eye-Catching Bibliographies (and patterns)
- Books to Recommend for Reading Aloud
- Sources of Stuffed Animals Based on Book Characters
- Sources of Contest Activities
- Sources of Inexpensive Prizes
- Companies that Provide Book Fairs
- Sources of Copyright-Free Clip Art
- Sources of Library Skills Games
- Sources of Reading Incentive Programs

EYE-CATCHING BIBLIOGRAPHIES

Displaying an eye-catching bibliography each month on your card catalog or check-out stand helps bring the books you want to feature to the students' attention. Write book titles and call numbers on symbols of the current month. For example, in October, copy enough pumpkins from the patterns provided for two pumpkins for each book. Use orange paper and outline one jack o'lantern in black. On the plain back of the other, write the book title and call number. Glue the two pumpkins back to back on the end of a tongue depressor. Make fifteen or twenty of these and display them in a decorated box or can on your card catalog or check-out desk. Change your bibliography each month. Save the old one for next year.

You can make genre-oriented bibliographies as well as seasonal bibliographies. For example, to make a bibliography of mystery books, cut out cardboard in the shape of a magnifying glass for the cover and back and pages from heavy paper or tagboard in the same shape. Write a title and call number on each page and bind them together with a single-ring binder. You can write a bibliography of dog books on bones cut from cardboard, and then display the bones in a plastic dog dish. A pattern for a dog bone bibliography is included, as well as a pattern for a cat story bibliography. You can write many bibliographies in this way—books about horses on horse-shaped paper, books about ghosts on ghost-shaped paper, and so on. If you have space, mount small cup hooks in a special area with the caption "Bibliographies," and hang the bibliographies with the ring binders.

BOOKS TO RECOMMEND
FOR READING ALOUD

Most classroom teachers in kindergarten or grade one have their favorite picture books to read aloud. Since picture books are short, teachers can come in and quickly browse and find books they would like to read. Beginning in grade two, when teachers read longer books, they often come in to ask your advice on what

HAPPY
NEW
YEAR!

books to read aloud to their class. Sometimes the request is made urgently, as in, "My class is waiting and I just finished the book I've been reading to them. What do you suggest?"

You probably know what books are suitable for each grade level. You probably have a sense of the kind of books each teacher prefers. If you are new to the school or just preoccupied, however, keeping a printed list near your desk is helpful. Here are some tried-and-true favorites. Add to the lists as you find others you like. Grade levels are not absolute, of course.

You may notice that there is at least one classic given for each grade level. Students need to be exposed to these classics because they are part of our heritage and culture. Also notice that most books at each grade level are either above most students' silent reading level or part of a series of books they might want to read. There are several Newbery winners included because students often enjoy these books more when they are read to them. The books listed are all well known, but you will find new books destined to become classics that you will want to add to your lists.

Grade Two

My Father's Dragon, by Ruth Gannett

The Boxcar Children, by Gertrude Chandler Warner

Charlotte's Web, by E. B. White

Ramona the Pest, by Beverly Cleary

Freckle Juice, by Judy Blume

King Midas and the Golden Touch, by Nathaniel Hawthorne, illustrated by Kathryn Hewitt, and *The Chocolate Touch,* by Patrick Catling. Read the original version before Catling's version.

Bunnicula, by James Howe

Winnie the Pooh, by A. A. Milne (Read the original—no condensed versions for read-alouds!)

OTHER TITLES YOU LIKE: _____

_____

_____

_____

_____

_____

_____

_____

Grade Three

James and the Giant Peach, by Roald Dahl

Runaway Ralph, by Beverly Cleary

Ellen Tebbits, by Beverly Cleary

Tales of a Fourth Grade Nothing, by Judy Blume

Chocolate Fever, by Robert Smith

The Wizard of Oz, by L. Frank Baum (Persuade a teacher to read this—there are many episodes not included in the movie!)

Little House in the Big Woods, by Laura Ingalls Wilder

The Borrowers, by Mary Norton

Alice's Adventures in Wonderland, by Lewis Carroll

Mrs. Piggle Wiggle, by Betty MacDonald

Tales of Olga da Polga, by Michael Bond

OTHER TITLES YOU LIKE: _____

_____

_____

_____

_____

_____

_____

_____

_____

Grade Four

The Black Stallion, by Walter Farley

Kavik the Wolf Dog, by Walt Morey

The T.V. Kid, by Betsy Byars

The Indian in the Cupboard, by Lynn Reid Banks

Owl in the Family, by Farley Mowat

The Rescuers, by Margery Sharp

Soup, by Robert Peck

Thirteen Ways to Sink a Sub, by Jamie Gilson

Bristle Face, by Zachary Ball

Kneeknock Rise, by Natalie Babbitt

The Secret Garden, by Frances Burnett

The Enormous Egg, by Oliver Butterworth

The Lion, the Witch and the Wardrobe, by C. S. Lewis

OTHER TITLES YOU LIKE: _____

_____

_____

_____

_____

_____

_____

_____

_____

_____

_____

Grade Five

Wait for Me, Watch for Me Eula Bee, by Patricia Beatty

House with a Clock in Its Walls, by John Bellairs

The Great Brain, by John Fitzgerald

Adventures of Tom Sawyer, by Mark Twain

My Brother Sam is Dead, by James and Lincoln Collier

Sasha My Friend, by Barbara Corcoran

Danny the Champion of the World, by Roald Dahl

Harriet, the Spy, by Louise Fitzhugh

From the Mixed Up Files of Mrs. Basil E. Frankweiler, by E. L. Konigsburg

Johnny Tremain, by Esther Forbes

Sandy and the Rock Star, by Walt Morey

On to Oregon, by Honoré Morrow

Mrs. Frisby and the Rats of NIMH, by Robert O'Brien

Bridge to Terabithia, by Katherine Paterson

Where the Red Fern Grows, by Wilson Rawls

The Egypt Game, by Zilpha Snyder

OTHER TITLES YOU LIKE: _____

_____

_____

_____

_____

_____

_____

Grade Six

The Cay, by Theodore Taylor

The Hobbit, or There and Back Again, by J. R. R. Tolkien

The Swiss Family Robinson, by Johann Wyss

Hans Brinker and the Silver Skates, by Mary Mapes Dodge

Call it Courage, by Armstrong Sperry

Roll of Thunder, Hear My Cry, by Mildred Taylor

The Book of Three, by Lloyd Alexander

The White Mountains, by John Christopher

The Dark is Rising, by Susan Cooper

A Christmas Carol, by Charles Dickens

Incident at Hawk's Hill, by Allan Eckert

Julie of the Wolves, by Jean George

Island of the Blue Dolphin, by Scott O'Dell

Treasure Island, by Robert Louis Stevenson

The Yearling, by Marjorie Kinnan Rawlings

The Upstairs Room, by Johanna Reiss

OTHER TITLES YOU LIKE: _____

_____

_____

_____

_____

_____

_____

SOURCES OF STUFFED ANIMALS
BASED ON BOOK CHARACTERS

LISTENING LIBRARY
One Park Avenue
Old Greenwich, CT 06870-1727

Peter Rabbit, Clifford, Babar, Curious George, and the Wild Thing are available in small and giant sizes. Other dolls available in small sizes are Humpty Dumpty, Spot, Pippie Longstocking, Mother Goose, and more.

THE HIGHSMITH COMPANY
W 5527 Highway 106
P.O. Box 800
Fort Atkinson, WI 53538-0800

The Wild Thing is also available from Highsmith. They also have many puppet characters that fit in well with storytimes.

UPSTART
32 East Avenue
Hagerstown, MD 21740

Humpty Dumpty and Mother Goose are two stuffed toys available from Upstart.

SOURCES OF CONTEST
ACTIVITIES

CHALLENGE Magazine
Box 299
Carthage, IL 62321-0299

QUAILRIDGE MEDIA
P.O. Box 328
Selma, OR 97538 (for Crossword Counts and Student Detective)

CREATIVE KIDS Magazine
P.O. Box 637
Holmes, PA 19043

THE CENTER FOR APPLIED RESEARCH IN EDUCATION
Prentice Hall Order Department
200 Old Tappan Road
Old Tappan, NJ 07675   (for Ready-to-Use Reading Bingos, Puzzles and Research Activities for Every Month of the Elementary School Year, and other helpful books)

OTHER SOURCES: _____

_____

_____

_____

—————— SOURCES OF INEXPENSIVE —————— PRIZES

ATLAS PEN & PENCIL CORPORATION
SCHOOL STORE DIVISION
3040 N. 29th Ave.
Hollywood, FL 33022

GOOD TIME ATTRACTIONS
8465 Plaza Blvd.
Spring Lake Park, MN 55432

UPSTART
32 East Avenue
Hagerstown, MD 21740

SMILEMAKERS
P.O. Box 2543
Spartanburg, SC 29304

ORIENTAL TRADING COMPANY, INC.
4206 South 108th St.
Omaha, NE 68137-1215

OTHER SOURCES: _____

_____

_____

_____

—————— COMPANIES THAT PROVIDE —————— BOOK FAIRS

GREAT AMERICAN BOOK FAIRS
2827-A 29th Avenue
P.O. Box 7649
Olympia, WA 98507

SCHOOL BOOK FAIRS
401 E. Wilson Bridge Road
Worthington, OH 43085-9970

TROLL BOOK FAIRS
100 Corporate Drive
Mahwah, NJ 07430

OTHER SOURCES: _____

_____

_____

_____

_____ *SOURCES OF COPYRIGHT-FREE* _____
CLIP ART

DOVER PUBLICATIONS, INC.
31 East 2nd Street
Mineola, NY 11501

Dover Publications publishes a number of books of clip art, borders on lay-out grids, and so on, most at very reasonable prices. Write for their catalog.

GOOD APPLE, INC.
Box 299
Carthage, IL 62321-0299

Good Apple publishes *Holidays, Seasons and Events Clip and Copy Art,* by Nancee McClure, and other sources as well.

HARTCO GRAPHIC SUPPLIES AND EQUIPMENT
West Jefferson, OH 43162

Their catalog is a source of clip art, borders, and so on.

OTHER SOURCES: _____

_____

_____

_____

SOURCES OF LIBRARY
SKILLS GAMES

BOOKWORM PRODUCTIONS
426 West 19th
McMinnville, OR 97128

Bookworm Productions is a source for class-size games such as Media Mania and Media Know Tic-Tac-Toe (reference, library terms, card catalog, parts of a book), Scavenger Hunt (research skills), Card Catalog Relay (card catalog), and Bookie Bookworm Puppet Kit (book care, card catalog).

DEMCO
Box 7767
Fresno, CA 93747

DEMCO produces Cool Chicken for 1 to 6 players (card catalog, Dewey Decimal system, dictionary, book parts, etc.) and Book Bug Game for 2 to 6 players (interest in books).

HIGHSMITH
W 5527 Highway 106
P.O. Box 800
Fort Atkinson, WI 53538-0800

Highsmith produces a number of games for a variety of groups, including Authors, Shelve-It, Roads to Knowledge, Caldecott Game, Newbery Game, Library Adventure Game, Where in the World? and Know Your America.

UPSTART
32 East Avenue
Hagerstown, MD 21740

Upstart produces Library Adventure Game, By Jove (mythology), Reado (Dewey Decimal System), and Fairytale Rummy.

THE CENTER FOR APPLIED RESEARCH IN EDUCATION
Prentice Hall Order Department
200 Old Tappan Road
Old Tappan, NJ 07675

C.A.R.E. publishes a number of books that contain library skills games, including *Library Games Activities Kit: Ready-to-Use Activities for Teaching Library Skills in 20 Minutes a Week,* by Patti Hulet, *Complete Library Skills Activities Program: Ready-to-Use Lessons for Grades K–6,* by Arden Druce, *Library Skills Activities for the Primary Grades,* by Ruth V. Snoddon, and *Hooked on Library*

Skills! A Sequential Activities Program for Grades K–6 as well as numerous other library resource books.

OTHER SOURCES: _____

_____

_____

_____

SOURCES OF READING INCENTIVE PROGRAMS

BOOKS AND BEYOND
Solana Beach School
309 N. Rios Avenue
Solana Beach, CA 92075

(eight levels of reading incentives; includes prizes, bookmarks, book report forms, etc.)

UPSTART
Box 889
Hagerstown, MD 21741-0889

(various seasonal reading incentive activities)

THE CENTER FOR APPLIED RESEARCH IN EDUCATION
Prentice Hall Order Department
200 Old Tappan Road
Old Tappan, NJ 07675

A variety of books containing reading incentive materials, including *Ready-to-Use Reading Bingos, Puzzles and Research Activities for Every Month of the Elementary School Year, Hooked on Reading!, Reading Activities for Every Month of the School Year, Reading Round-Ups*, and more.

WORLD BOOK, INC.
525 W. Monroe St.
Chicago, IL 60606

"Partners in Excellence" program encourages students to read as they earn encyclopedias, science sets, and dictionaries for their school and classroom.

OTHER SOURCES: _____

_____

_____

_____

A

Aardema, Verna, 115
Alexandra, The Rock-Eater (Woerkam), 115
Allard, Harry, 25
Almanac practice, 94
Anastasia on Her Own (Lowry), 156
Annie Bananie (Komaiko), 25
April, 163–83
Arthur's Halloween (Brown), 55
Arthur's Thanksgiving (Brown), 78
Arthur's Valentine (Brown), 138
Arts and crafts corner
  April, 170
  December, 90, 92
  February, 133
  January, 109, 112
  March, 152
  May, 191
  November, 73–74
  October, 46, 48, 49
  September, 19–20
Asch, Frank, 24
Audiovisual area, 5
Audiovisual equipment
  check-out, 79–80
  repair, 221
  scheduling, 5
  training, 58–59
Authors' birthday club
  April, 167–69
  December, 87–89
  February, 129–31
  January, 107–9
  March, 150, 151
  May, 189, 190
  November, 70–72
  October, 43–45
  September, 11–16
  summer, 215, 217–18, 219–20
Authors' visits, 96–97

B

Balian, Lorna, 138
Bang, Molly, 51
Banks, Lynne Reid, 117
Best Christmas Pageant Ever, The (Robinson), 95
Bibliographies, 228
Big Splash Birthday Bash (Noble), 201
Black History Month, 127
Bony Legs (Cole), 51
Book fairs, 157–58, 236–37
Books Are for Eating (Walton), 177

Book talks
  April, 177–78
  December, 95–96
  February, 140
  March, 156–57
  May, 202
  November, 78–79
  October, 55–56
  September, 26–27
Brave Irene (Steig), 78
Brink, Carol Ryrie, 79
Brown, Marc, 55, 78, 138
Bulletin boards
  April, 166–67
  December, 86–87
  February, 128–29
  January, 105–6
  June, 213–14
  May, 187–89
  November, 69–70
  October, 42–43
  September, 10–11
Burning Questions of Bingo Brown, The (Byars), 202
Butter Battle Book, The (Seuss), 155
Byars, Betsy, 202

C

Caddie Woodlawn (Brink), 79
Caldecott books, 176–78
Calendar
  April, 164
  December, 84
  February, 126
  January, 102
  June, 212
  March, 146
  May, 186
  November, 66
  October, 38
  September, 2
Call number slips, 51, 52, 76, 93, 114, 137, 174, 175
Calmenson, Stephanie, 115
Card catalog, 4
  filing, 141
  practice cards, 51, 53–54
Catalogs, 2, 80, 221
Chicken Little (Kellogg), 115
Chinese New Year, 105, 106
Christina's Ghost (Wright), 202
Christmas, 95–96
Christmas Wolf, The (Gay), 95
Classes, scheduling, 5–6
Cleary, Beverly, 26

Clip art, sources, 237
Cole, Joanna, 51
Company's Coming (Yorinks), 201
Computer systems, 203–4
Conford, Ellen, 157
Contest corner
  April, 169–70
  December, 89–90
  February, 131–33
  January, 109
  March, 150, 152
  May, 189, 191
  November, 72–73
  October, 46, 47
  September, 17–19
  sources, 235–36
Corbett, Scott, 55, 56
Costikyan, Barbara Heine, 95, 96
Crossword puzzle, 89–90, 91

D

Day the Teacher Went Bananas, The (Howe), 25
December, 83–100
DeClements, Barthe, 26
Dewey Decimal system, 75, 77
Dictionary practice, 40, 94
Disappearing Bag, The (Wells), 95
Doctor DeSoto (Steig), 78
Dollhouse Murders, The (Wright), 55
Donations, 178–80
Doorbell Rang, The (Hutchins), 20
Double Dog Dare (Gilson), 202

E

Easy section, 4
Edmonds, Walter, 79
Encyclopedia Brown, Boy Detective (Sobol), 56
Engel, Diana, 177

F

Fairy tale/fantasy
  activities, 103–4, 110–11
  arts and crafts corner, 112
  book talk, 117–18
  bulletin board, 105–6
  contest corner, 109
  skills class, 113, 114
  storytime, 115, 117
Fat Cat (Kent), 24
Fiction section, 4
Filing, 141
Fitzgerald, John D., 140

G

Gackenbach, Dick, 51
Galdone, Paul, 24, 115, 201
Games area, 5

Garden of Abduhl Gazazi, The (Van Allsburg), 176
Gay, Michael, 95
Gilson, Jamie, 26, 202
Goblins'll Get You, The (Whittier), 55
Great Brain, The (Fitzgerald), 140
Greenburg, Sheila, 26

H

Halloween, 39, 46, 51, 53, 54, 55
Hamilton, Virginia, 157
Haunted House (Pienkowski), 55
Haywood, Carolyn, 138
Herschel and the Hanukah Goblins (Kimmel), 95, 96
Historical fiction, 78–79
Hobyahs, The (Parks and Smith), 55
Horton Hatches the Egg (Seuss), 155
House of Dies Drear, The (Hamilton), 157
House Without a Christmas Tree, The (Rock), 95
Houston, Gloria, 95
How to Eat Fried Worms (Rockwell), 156
Howe, James, 25
Huck, Charlotte, 115
Hutchins, Pat, 55, 201

I

Iceberg and Its Shadow, The (Greenburg), 26
Illustrators' visits, 97
Indian in the Cupboard, The (Banks), 117
Inventory, 221
It's Christmas (Prelutsky), 95

J

January, 101–23
Jimmy's Boa (Noble), 201
Josephina Hates Her Name (Engel), 177
Judge, The (Zemach), 176–77
June, 211–25

K

Kellogg, Steven, 115
Kent, Jack, 24, 156
Kimmel, Eric, 95, 96
King Bidgood's in the Bathtub (Wood), 176
King (Martin Luther, Jr.) Day, 105
Komaiko, Leah, 25
Krause, Ute, 138, 140

L

Lady with the Alligator Purse, The (Westcott), 138
Lauber, Patricia, 140
Levitin, Sonia, 79
Librarian's station, 5
Liza Lou and the Yeller Belly Swamp (Mayer), 51
Lon Po Po, 115
Lowry, Lois, 140, 156

M

McElligot's Pool (Seuss), 155
Magazines, 2, 178
Maggie Forevermore (Nixon), 96
Map practice, 94
March, 145–61
Marshall, James, 115
Matchlock Gun, The (Edmonds), 79
Max's Chocolate Chicken (Wells), 177
Max's Christmas (Wells), 95
May, 185–209
Mayer, Mercer, 51
Me and the Terrible Two (Conford), 157
Miss Nelson Has a Field Day (Allard), 25
Monkey and the Crocodile, The (Galdone), 24
Monkey Face (Asch), 24
Mother's Day Sandwich, The (Wynot), 201
Munsch, Robert, 115
Mystery books, 55–56

N

National Children's Book Week, 67
National Education Week, 68
National Library Week, 165, 169, 170, 171, 176
Newberry books, 178
Nixon, Joan Lowery, 96
Noble, Trinka Hakes, 201
Nonfiction corner, 4
   April, 170–71
   December, 92
   February, 133–34
   January, 112–13
   March, 152–53
   May, 192
   November, 74
   October, 48, 50
   September, 20–21
Nothing's Fair in Fifth Grade (DeClements), 26
November, 65–82
Number the Stars (Lowry), 140

O

October, 37–63
One Hundredth Thing About Caroline, The (Lowry),
   156–57
Ordering, 3–4, 24, 80, 118, 221–22
Orientation class, 21–22
Overdue books, 58, 220

P

Paperbag Princess, The (Munsch), 115
Parent volunteers, 27, 28
Parks, B., 55
Peck, Robert, 140
Pienkowski, Jan, 55
Pierre (Sendak), 138
Pig Surprise (Krause), 138, 140

Plan
   monthly, 8
   overall, 6, 7
Poetry, 85
Polar Express, The (Van Allsburg), 95, 96
Prelutsky, Jack, 25, 95
Presidents Day, 127, 129, 132, 133
Princess Furball (Huck), 115
Principal's New Clothes, The (Calmenson), 115
Prizes, 18–19, 72, 236
Processing system, 3–4
Publishing books, 153–55

Q

Quotations, finding, 134–36

R

Ramona the Pest (Cleary), 26
Reading aloud
   books, 228, 231–34
   file cards, 25
   See also Storytimes
Reading programs
   read-away airlines, 194–220
   sources, 239
   summer, 215–20
Red Room Riddle, The (Corbett), 55, 56
Reference section, 4
Reiss, Joanna, 79
Research questions, 21, 48, 50, 74, 92, 112, 134, 153,
   170–71, 192
Roanoke (Levitin), 79
Robinson, Barbara, 95
Rock, Gail, 95
Rockwell, Thomas, 156
Rolling Harvey Down the Hill (Prelutsky), 25

S

San Souci, Robert, 176
Scavenger hunt, 23, 24, 171–74
Scheduling, 5–6
Sendak, Maurice, 138
September, 1–36
Seuss, Dr., 95, 147, 150, 155–56
Sign of the Beaver, The (Speare), 78
Skills classes
   April, 171–76
   December, 93, 94
   February, 134–38
   January, 113, 114
   March, 153–55
   May, 192–94
   November, 75–77
   October, 51, 52–54
   September, 21–24
   sources of games, 238–39
Smith, J., 55

Sneetches, The (Seuss), 155
Sobol, Donald J., 56
Soup (Peck), 140
Speare, Elizabeth, 78
Special areas, 4–5
Special day ideas
  April, 165
  December, 85–86
  February, 127–28
  January, 105
  March, 147–48
  May, 187
  November, 67–68
  October, 40–42
  September, 9
Steig, William, 78
Storytimes, 4
  April, 176–77
  December, 94–95
  February, 138, 140
  January, 115–17
  March, 155–56
  May, 201
  November, 78
  October, 51, 55
  September, 24
  See also Reading aloud
Student volunteers, 27, 29–32, 58
Stuffed animals, book character, 235
Summer reading, 215–20
Sweetheart for a Valentine, A (Balian), 138
Sylvester and the Magic Pebble (Steig), 78

T

Talking Eggs, The (San Souci), 176
Teachers, contacts with, 118
Teaching area, 4
Themes
  April, 165
  December, 85
  February, 127
  January, 103–4, 110–11
  June, 213
  March, 147

Themes (*cont'd*)
  May, 187
  November, 67
  October, 39
  September, 6, 9
13 Ways to Sink a Sub (Gilson), 26
Three Sillies, The (Galdone), 201

U

Upstairs Room, The (Reiss), 79

V

Valentine Fantasy, A (Haywood), 138
Valentine's Day, 127, 128, 132, 133, 134, 135, 136, 138
Van Allsburg, Chris, 95, 96, 118, 176, 177
Volcano (Lauber), 140
Volunteers
  parent, 27, 28
  student, 27, 29–32, 58
  thanking, 222

W

Walton, Sherry, 177
Weeding, 141–42, 220–21
Wells, Rosemary, 95, 177
Westcott, Nadine Bernard, 138
Where's the Baby (Hutchins), 55
Whittier, John Greenleaf, 55
Wiley and the Hairy Man (Bang), 51
Woerkam, Van, 115
Wood, Audrey, 176
Worksheets, 75
Wright, Betty Ren, 55, 202
Wynot, Jillian, 201

Y

Year of the Perfect Christmas Tree, The (Houston), 95
Yertle the Turtle (Seuss), 155
Yorinks, Arthur, 201

Z

Zemach, Harve, 176–77